THE GOSPEL OF THE KINGDOM

THE GOSPEL
OF THE
KINGDOM

*God's Eternal Purpose
in Christ*

JON VON ERNST

AVAILABLE AS AUDIOBOOK

XULON PRESS

Xulon Press
2301 Lucien Way #415
Maitland, FL 32751
407.339.4217
www.xulonpress.com

The Gospel of the Kingdom
God's Eternal Purpose in Christ

Paperback ISBN-13: 978-1-6628-1735-9
Ebook ISBN-13: 978-1-6628-1736-6

Correspondence may be addressed to the author at:
thepureword@yahoo.com

Dedication

All Your works will give thanks to You, LORD,
And Your godly ones will bless You.
They will speak of the glory of Your kingdom,
And talk of Your might,
To make known to the sons of mankind Your mighty acts,
And the glory of the majesty of Your kingdom.
Your kingdom is an everlasting kingdom,
And Your dominion endures throughout all generations.
The LORD is faithful in His words,
And holy in all His works.

The LORD is righteous in all His ways,
And kind in all His works.
The LORD is near to all who call on Him,
To all who call on Him in truth.
He will fulfill the desire of those who fear Him;
He will also hear their cry for help and save them.
The LORD watches over all who love Him,
But He will destroy all the wicked.
My mouth will speak the praise of the LORD,
And all flesh will bless His holy name forever and ever.
The LORD watches over all who love him,
But all the wicked he will destroy.
My mouth will speak in praise of the LORD.
Let every creature praise His holy name for ever and ever.

Psalm 145:10-13, 17-21

Contents

Preface vii

Introduction. xi

The Gospel of the Kingdom 1

Obedience to the Gospel 12

Receiving the Promises. 20

Full Salvation 31

Assurance of Salvation 42

Everything You Need 48

A God of Order 58

The Mind-set of the Spirit. 67

Love and Forgiveness 75

God's Eternal Purpose in Christ 84

The Unity of the Spirit 94

Trusting the Holy Spirit 100

Counterfeit Churches 106

The Antichrists 114

Come Out of Her, My People 120

Life after Death. 127

The Lake of Fire 133

The Great White Throne Judgment. 139

Test Yourself 146

Bowing the Knee. 153

Preface

Two essential truths are sadly lacking in many churches today. The first is the absolute necessity of being born again, of having the Spirit of Christ. The second is the absolute necessity of confessing Jesus as Lord and entering into a relationship with Him in the full knowledge of and submission to His place as the supreme authority in the believer's life.

Jesus has won the victory! Through His death on the cross and by the power of His resurrection from the dead, Jesus has defeated the one holding the power of death, the Devil, so those who were held in slavery all their lives by the fear of death might be set free (Hebrews 2:14-15).

Seeing everyone walking around wearing face masks only amplifies this fear as the world is terrorized by the thought of becoming sick and dying. This terrorized population is willing to do anything they are told, if only they might live another day. This is the picture of a world without God, a world without hope (Ephesians 2:11-12).

This world is a kingdom of darkness, pain, sorrow, fear, and death. However, because of the victory that Jesus has won, every person in this dark world now has an opportunity to be set free from the bondage of this kingdom of darkness and be transferred into God's kingdom of love, light, joy, and peace, with the promise of everlasting life. This is the good news. This is the gospel of the kingdom, the spiritual kingdom of God (Colossians 1:11-14).

The gospel of the kingdom is good news for bad people! It shows the way out of the darkness and fear of this world and into the light and love of the kingdom of God. This way has been opened so that any person, no matter what they have done, who they are, or where they are from, may be set free to enter this glorious new kingdom of light. The blood of Jesus Christ shed on the cross is sufficient to satisfy the righteousness of God and to cleanse us from all sin. Now, every person that repents, turning back to God by faith in Jesus and is born again, born of the Spirit, is transferred into this wonderful kingdom of God (Acts 2:38-40).

Jesus came into the world to save sinners (I Timothy 1:15). Jesus said, "There will be more joy in heaven over one sinner who repents than over ninety-nine righteous people who have no need of repentance" (Luke 15:7). When you repent, turning from your sinful past unto God by faith in Jesus Christ, not only do you experience real lasting joy for the first time in your life, but you also cause great rejoicing in heaven.

The gospel of the kingdom is also bad news for good people! Scripture makes it clear that no matter what we have done by our own strength and according to our own under-standing in service to God and in the name of the Lord, it will never be sufficient to open the way for us to enter the kingdom of God. Only those that do the will of God the Father will enter into the kingdom of God.

Jesus said, "Not everyone who says to Me, 'Lord, Lord,' will enter the kingdom of heaven, but the one who does the will of My Father who is in heaven will enter. Many will say to Me on that day, 'Lord, Lord, did we not prophesy in Your name, and in Your name cast out demons, and in Your name perform many miracles?' And then I will declare to them, 'I never knew you; LEAVE ME, YOU WHO PRACTICE LAWLESSNESS.'" (Matthew 7:21-23).

Jesus said, "No one can enter the kingdom of God unless they are born of water and the Spirit" (John 3:5-6). Every person living today has been born of water through child-birth into the kingdom of this world, a material kingdom. We can only enter the spiritual kingdom of God by being born again, born from above, born of the Spirit.

The singular importance of the Holy Spirit in the believer's life is extensively discussed in my previous book, *The Victorious Christian – Inheriting the Promises*. You cannot be a genuine Christian without being born again. If you do not have the Spirit of Christ, you do not belong to Him, you are not a genuine Christian (Romans 8:9).

If you have repented, believing in Jesus, but have not received the Holy Spirit, do not be discouraged. God wants to give His Holy Spirit to you. Jesus said, "So if you, despite being evil, know how to give good gifts to your children, how much more will your heavenly Father give the Holy Spirit to those who ask Him?" All you need to do is exercise your faith by asking the Father, persisting, believing, and God will give the Spirit to you (Luke 11:9-13). We need to remember that God gives His Spirit to those that obey Him (Acts 5:32).

However, being born again, receiving the Holy Spirit, is not the end, it is only the beginning of the salvation experience. Upon being born again, it is essential that we make a public confession of our new life in the Spirit and of our allegiance to Jesus as Lord, as the supreme authority in our life. This is the most important thing that each person needs to understand after being born again. God causes us to be born again that we might be separated from the world unto Himself. Our public confession plays a significant role in this process. (Matthew 10:32-33).

When God sets us apart unto Himself, He brings us out of our old relationships in the world and places us into the body of Christ, the church. God places us in the body of Christ, as it pleases Him, to be built up together with other believers. He commands us to love these brothers and sisters in Christ that He has placed us with (John 13:34).

God expects us to encourage each other in the faith, to build up the church, the body of Christ. He enables us to do this by listening to and obeying the leading of the indwelling Holy Spirit. He empowers us to live holy lives by being led by His Spirit (Galatians 5:16-25). This joyful submission to Jesus Christ as Lord, by yielding to the leading of His indwelling Spirit, is essential to enter into the fullness of God's eternal purpose in Christ (I Peter 1:3-9).

By the power of the resurrection from the dead, Jesus has been made to be both Lord and Christ. All authority has been given unto Him. This is the essence of the gospel of the kingdom. This is what the apostles bore witness to. This is the gospel we must believe. This is the gospel we must proclaim (Matthew 28:18-20, Acts 2:32-36, Romans 10:8-10). Jesus said, "This gospel of the kingdom shall be preached in the whole world as a testimony to all the nations, and then the end will come" (Matthew 24:14).

This book presents these truths in practical applications for our individual Christian lives and for our corporate church life to encourage believers to walk in faithful obedience to the leading of the Holy Spirit. God is glorified as we demonstrate our love for Him through our obedience and through our love for one another, encouraging each other to gladly suffer for Christ and to endure faithfully to the end.

This book has been designed as a resource for Bible study for both individuals and groups. There are discussion questions at the end of each chapter. These questions are intended to stimulate thought and discussion concerning the truths covered in each chapter and how they apply to our lives. It is my hope that they will help each reader come to a deeper understanding of our God and of His ways.

Jon von Ernst

Introduction

It is important that the reader understand the danger of accepting the teachings of this author, or any other author, pastor, or teacher at face value. No person's teachings should be blindly accepted. When we, without question, accept anyone's teachings we place ourselves in danger of being led astray. There are many false teachers in the world and in the church today. It is essential that we try the spirits, and that we take any teaching, no matter how famous or highly revered the teacher may be, to the Scriptures for verification. This author encourages you to take the teachings of this book to the Scriptures and search them out diligently.

When we take teachings to the Scriptures, it is important to look up and review the context of the passages that the teacher has referred to. It may be even more important to allow the Spirit to direct us to passages that appear to contradict the conclusions presented by the teacher. Usually there is more than one perspective presented in Scripture for any individual truth. This is due to the incredible depth of the manifold wisdom of God. It is the tendency of natural man to see, at most, only one side of any truth presented in Scripture. It is therefore necessary for the reader, the listener, to look to the Holy Spirit to reveal more than just one aspect of any truth in question. We should desire God to reveal to us as many aspects of the specific truth as He is willing to show us, and that we are able and prepared to receive.

Our initial desire in searching out in the Scriptures the truths that are being taught is to verify if the teachings do in fact have a Scriptural basis and are properly applied. Our secondary goal is to broaden our understanding of the specific truth being taught by seeing that truth from other perspectives, thereby deepening our understanding of our God and of His ways. As we come to see various aspects of any truth, we will become more accepting of other believers, and of their individual understanding of the truths that they have come to believe and embrace. This will enable us to more effectively maintain the unity of the Spirit and to reduce the tendency to separate ourselves from other believers simply because we have stumbled upon some teaching about which there are different understandings.

It is important for all of us to realize that none of us has all understanding or all knowledge of the truths presented in Scripture. At best, we see in part and we understand in part. We are all disciples. We are all students. We are all in the process of learning. The only way any of us can learn is if we begin by humbling ourselves and admit that we don't have all the answers. We need to consider others as better than ourselves and realize that if we have an ear to hear, God can teach us by His Spirit through the speaking of any brother or sister. When we think too highly of ourselves, we have greatly reduced our ability to learn.

Our ultimate goal in coming to the Scriptures is to be fed. We must come to the Scriptures as those that are hungry for the living word of God, Jesus Christ our Lord. Our desire should be to know Him. May God give us the grace and the hunger to hear God's speaking by His Spirit through the Scriptures and through every brother and sister that we fellowship with. Perhaps if we are hungry enough, God will feed us with more of Christ, that at His return, we may know Him and be found in Him!

May we be those that are truly taught by the Holy Spirit and not by men.

Jon von Ernst

The Gospel of the Kingdom

H ave you ever realized that there is more to this world you live in then what you can see, touch, taste, smell or hear? Beyond the material world that we are continually aware of by use of our five senses, there is a spiritual world, a world just as real as this material one.

In this spiritual world that surrounds us, there are many beings, many creatures busy at work, just as we are in our material world. But what are these creatures so busy doing? Just as in our material world, many of them are involved in a battle, a spiritual warfare. This war started long before our material world was even created, and it continues today, all around us. In fact, we, you and I, are what this spiritual war is all about.

Before the earth was even formed, God, who is spirit, created angels, spiritual beings, to serve Him (Job 1:6, 38:4-7). One of the highest of these angels was made by God to be "full of wisdom, and perfect in beauty" (Ezekiel 28:12-13, KJV). He was given a position of honor, ministering on "the holy mountain of God" (Ezekiel 28:14, KJV).

However, lifted up with pride, this angel rebelled against God, saying in his heart, "I will ascend to heaven; I will raise my throne above the stars of God, I will ascend above the heights of the clouds; I will make myself like the Most High" (Isaiah 14:13-14). God, speaking in the book of Ezekiel, says of him, "You sinned; therefore I have cast you as profane from the mountain of God...Your heart was lifted up because of your beauty; you corrupted your wisdom by reason of your splendor. I cast you to the ground" (Ezekiel 28:16-17).

1

In his attempt to establish his own kingdom and set himself up as God, this angel led many of the other angels away with him (Revelation 12:9). This angel, who goes by many names, (e.g. Satan, Lucifer, the devil), has ever since been at war, he and his angels that followed him, against God and His angels that continued to serve Him. This is the spiritual warfare. What does this spiritual war have to do with us?

When God created man, He placed him in the garden of Eden, a garden full of many kinds of trees. In the midst of this garden, God caused two very special trees to grow, the tree of life and the tree of the knowledge of good and evil. God commanded the man saying that he could freely eat of any tree in the garden, except from the tree of the knowledge of good and evil. He was giving man the opportunity to choose whether or not he would obey God and live under his authority, or rebel as Satan had (Genesis 2:8-9, 16-17).

Satan then came to the garden, in the form of a serpent, spoke to the woman, deceived her and caused her to eat of the forbidden fruit of the tree of the knowledge of good and evil. Then she gave the fruit to the man, and he chose to rebel against God and join his wife in sin by eating of the forbidden fruit. In God's righteous judgment on man's sin, God blocked the way to the tree of life that man could not eat of it and live forever. God sent man out of the garden and blocked the way to eternal life and the kingdom of God. Satan had apparently gained a great victory in this first battle for the soul of man (Genesis 3:1-6, 22-24).

According to the Bible, all of mankind has fallen into the snare of the devil, Satan, and has been taken captive by him at his will. 2 Timothy 2:24-26 says, "The Lord's bond-servant must not be quarrelsome, but be kind to all, able to teach, patient when wronged, with gentleness correcting those who are in opposition, if perhaps God may grant them repentance leading to the knowledge of the truth, and they may come to their senses and escape from the snare of the devil, having been held captive by him to do his will."

Romans 3:23 says, "All have sinned and fall short of the glory of God." Romans 6:23 tells us that "the wages of sin is death" (KJV). Therefore, all men must die. We are all held in bondage to Satan by the power of sin and death in our lives. The whole world lies in the evil one, under his power, in bondage to him, forced to do his will. 1 John 5:19 declares that "the whole world lies in the power of the evil one." What a hopeless situation!

It seemed God's one chance to free mankind from Satan's deadly grasp was to send his only Son into the world. However, God was not surprised by this situation. This was, in fact, God's plan before the foundation of the earth (I Peter 1:18-21). The only surprise was that Satan was unaware of God's plan.

The Son was the exact expression of God, the very essence of His being. God, who is spirit, sent the Son into this material world that we live in, in the likeness of sinful flesh, in the form of a man (Philippians 2:6-8). He trusted His Son to live a life in this sinful world, yet without sin and in complete obedience to Him (Hebrews 4:15). While we were without hope in this world, God sent His Son to deliver us from Satan's power (Romans 5:6; Ephesians 2:12).

Satan, however, being unaware of God's plan, thought that now, with the only Son of God in a body of flesh, all he had to do was kill the Son, and he would finally win the battle by destroying the Son of God, God's king, Jesus (Matthew 21:37-38). With the Son dead, everything would belong to Satan, and all of the world would worship him.

So Satan had Jesus, the Son of God, put to death on a cross. However, what the enemy meant for evil, God worked for good. Satan did not understand the wisdom of God, for if he had understood it, he would not have crucified Jesus. 1 Corinthians 2:8 says, "We speak God's wisdom in a mystery...the wisdom which none of the rulers of this age has understood; for if they had understood it they would not have crucified the Lord of glory."

By His death on the cross, Jesus broke the power of death, the master weapon of Satan's kingdom, because death was not able to hold Him (Acts 2:24). By His resurrection from the dead, Jesus defeated the enemy, making an open display of him, triumphing over him in it (Colossians 2:15; 1 Corinthians 15:55-57). Hebrews 2:14-15 speaks of Jesus' victory over Satan saying, "Therefore, since the children share in flesh and blood, He Himself likewise also partook of the same, that through death He might render powerless him who had the power of death, that is, the devil, and might free those who through fear of death were subject to slavery all their lives."

This is good news! Jesus has won the victory! By the power of His resurrection, He has set us free! By believing that God raised Jesus from the dead and confessing Jesus as Lord, anyone can enter into His kingdom and enjoy all its riches, all of its promises and all of its blessings for life in this world and for life in the coming age.

God's righteous judgment of man's sin had blocked the way to the tree of life and the entrance into the kingdom of God. However, God, by His great love for mankind, provided us with a way back to Himself. This way is Jesus Christ the Lord. Romans 5:8-11 tells us, "God demonstrates His own love toward us, in that while we were yet sinners, Christ died for us. Much more then, having now been justified by His blood, we shall be saved from the wrath *of God* through Him. For if while we were enemies we were reconciled to God through the death of His Son, much more, having been reconciled, we shall be saved by His life. And not only this, but we also exult in God through our Lord Jesus Christ, through whom we have now received the reconciliation."

Jesus said in John14:6, "I am the way, the truth and the life; no one comes to the Father but through Me." Jesus is the only way back to God. He is the only way anyone can enter the kingdom of God. Jesus is the only way to receive eternal life, because He is the life. God, in His great love for us has provided a way, the only way, back to Himself by faith in Jesus, by complete submission to Him as Lord. God does not want any to perish, but for all to come to repentance, turning back from their sinful ways and returning to Him by faith in Jesus (2 Peter 3:9).

This is the good news, the gospel, of the kingdom! By His Love for us, God has opened the way for anyone, no matter who you are or what you have done, to turn back to God and to be reconciled to Him, by trusting in and submitting to Jesus as your Lord and King. Only by complete submission to God's King can anyone enter the Kingdom of God. Jesus invites everyone saying, "Come to Me, all who are weary and heavy-laden, and I will give you rest. Take My yoke upon you and learn from Me, for I am gentle and humble in heart, and YOU WILL FIND REST FOR YOUR SOULS. For My yoke is easy and My burden is light" (Matthew 11:28-30).

This is the gospel of the kingdom as presented in the Bible. Jesus came proclaiming this "gospel of the kingdom" (Matthew 4:23; 9:35; Mark 1:14-15). He said this "gospel of the kingdom shall be preached in the whole world...then the end shall come" (Matthew 24:14). After His death and resurrection, Jesus sent His disciples out to preach this gospel.

He did this, because all authority and power had been given unto Him, He had won the victory. He told His disciples "All authority has been given unto Me in heaven and on earth. Go therefore and make disciples of all the nations" (Matthew 28:18-19). In effect, He was saying to His disciples, go and teach all nations that I have been made Lord of all.

We can see, from the first proclamation of the gospel by the apostles in Acts chapter 2, that this is exactly what they understood Jesus' command to mean. On the day of Pentecost, the fiftieth day after the resurrection of Jesus, Peter stood and proclaimed in Jerusalem, "Men of Israel, listen to these words: Jesus the Nazarene, a man attested to you by God with miracles and wonders and signs which God performed through Him in your midst, just as you yourselves know–this Man, delivered over by the predetermined plan and foreknowledge of God, you nailed to a cross by the hands of godless men and put Him to death. But God raised Him up again, putting an end to the agony of death, since it was impossible for Him to be held in its power" (Acts 2:22-23).

Peter continued saying, "This Jesus God raised up again, to which we are all witnesses. Therefore having been exalted to the right hand of God, and having received from the Father the promise of the Holy Spirit, He has poured forth this which you both see and hear" (Acts 2:32-33). Peter concluded his message in verse 36 declaring, "Therefore let all the house of Israel know for certain that God has made Him both Lord and Christ–this Jesus whom you crucified." When Peter preached the gospel of the kingdom, he clearly understood it was altogether a matter of the Lordship of Jesus the Christ, evidenced by God having raised Him from the dead.

Jesus said, "Destroy this temple, and in three days I will raise it up" (John 2:19). He was speaking of the temple of His body (John 2:21). When God raised Jesus from the dead, not allowing his body to decay (Acts 2:27, 31), God was, by raising Him from the dead, placing His seal of approval on Jesus' life and death. Jesus lived a holy life, a sinless life, in order that by His death, He might pay the full price for our sins. He would, thereby, become our Savior, delivering us from all our sins.

However, if God had not raised Him from the dead, His death for our sins would have been meaningless. We would still be in our sins. Paul writes in 1 Corinthians 15:17, "If Christ has not been raised, your faith is worthless; you are still in your sins." It was by raising Jesus from the dead that God was declaring to the universe that Jesus' life and death were not only acceptable to God, but in them, He was wholly

6

satisfied. The resurrection was God's seal of approval. By it, God affirmed to the universe that Jesus was all He had claimed to be.

Jesus claimed to be the Son of God. The Jews understood rightly that by this He was declaring himself to be God (John 10:30, 33, 36). The apostle Paul says in Romans 1:4 that Jesus Christ our Lord "was declared the Son of God with power by the resurrection from the dead."

Jesus claimed to be the Christ (John 10:24-25). Peter says that, by the resurrection, God made Jesus to be both Lord and Christ (Acts 2:32, 36). That is, by raising Jesus from the dead, God confirmed that He, Jesus, was truly the Christ, the promised, anointed ruler prophesied throughout the Bible. He was the one who God said would eventually defeat Satan, the Serpent. (Genesis 3:15).

When we share the gospel of the kingdom, our message must focus on the person of Jesus, raised from the dead and made by God to be both Lord and Christ. We are to preach Jesus, and the kingdom of God just as the apostles did in the book of Acts.

In Acts 2:14-40 Peter said, "This Jesus God raised up again, to which we are all witnesses...know for certain that God has made Him both Lord and Christ, this Jesus whom you crucified." In Acts 3:11-26 Peter proclaims the name of Jesus saying, "On the basis of faith in His name, it is the name of Jesus which has strengthened this man whom you see and know."

In Acts 4:1-4 Peter was "proclaiming in Jesus the resurrection from the dead." In Acts 4:8-12 Peter declares "there is salvation in no one else; for there is no other name under heaven that has been given among men by which we must be saved." In Acts 4:33 the apostles were "giving testimony to the resurrection of the Lord Jesus." In Acts 5:29-32 Peter and the apostles proclaimed, "The God of our fathers raised up Jesus, whom you had put to death by hanging Him on a cross. He is the one whom God exalted to His right hand."

In Acts 8:12 Philip was "preaching the good news about the kingdom of God and the name of Jesus Christ." In Acts 10:34-46 Peter was "preaching peace through Jesus Christ (He is Lord of all)." In Acts 13:16-49 Paul declared, "We preach to you the good news of the promise made to the fathers, that God has fulfilled this promise to our children in that He raised up Jesus." In Acts 16:25-34 Paul and Silas proclaimed, "Believe in the Lord Jesus, and you will be saved, you and your household."

In Acts 17:16-34 Paul declares that God has "fixed a day in which He will judge the world in righteousness having furnished proof to all men by raising Him from the dead." In Acts 19:1-7 Paul says, "John baptized with the baptism of repentance, telling the people to believe in Him who was coming after him, that is, in Jesus." In Acts 28:23 Paul was "explaining to them by solemnly testifying about the kingdom of God and trying to persuade them concerning Jesus." In Acts 28:30-31 Paul was "preaching the kingdom of God and teaching concerning the Lord Jesus Christ."

When we preach this gospel, declaring that Jesus is Lord and that all authority has been given unto Him, those that hear this message will be challenged. If they believe our message, they will be compelled to obey by submitting to the authority of Jesus as Lord. If they do not obey the gospel, they are condemned already and the wrath of God abides on them. John 3:36 says, "He who believes in the Son has eternal life; but he who does not obey the Son will not see life, but the wrath of God abides on him." He who believes has the promise of inheriting eternal life if they remain faithful and endure to the end.

Having now heard this gospel of the kingdom, you have the opportunity to decide whether you will believe it and receive Jesus as your Lord and Master, or whether you will reject this gospel, reject the Lordship of Jesus in your life, and continue to serve Satan.

If you believe in your heart that God did indeed raise Jesus from the dead, and if you then, upon believing, confess Jesus as Lord, freely, willingly submitting to Him as the supreme authority, you will be saved (Romans 10:9-10). You will then be transferred, by being born again, into the kingdom of the King of kings. Colossians 1:13 says, "For He rescued us from the domain of darkness and transferred us to the kingdom of His beloved Son, in whom we have redemption, the forgiveness of sins."

The word "believe" means to be persuaded of something. It means to consider the facts, weigh the evidence, and then put your trust, your confidence in what has been proven to you to be true. Are you persuaded that God raised Jesus from the dead? Will you confess Him as Lord?

Jesus says, "Every one therefore who shall confess Me before men, I will also confess him before My Father who is in heaven. But whoever shall deny Me before men, I will also deny him before My Father who is in heaven" (Matthew 10:32-33). This word, translated as "deny" here, means "to not confess." To confess means to acknowledge. Do you acknowledge Jesus as Lord before men? If you do not acknowledge Him as Lord before men, He will not acknowledge you as His own before His Father in heaven.

Ephesians 6:11-12 says, "Put on the whole armor of God, so that you will be able to stand firm against the schemes of the devil. For our struggle is not against flesh and blood, but against the rulers, against the powers, against the world forces of this darkness, against the spiritual forces of wickedness in the heavenly places."

Now, today, these two kingdoms are engaged in a battle. They are in a spiritual warfare. They are fighting, warring for the souls of the people living on the earth. The one kingdom is the kingdom of light, the kingdom of God, whose king is Jesus. The other kingdom is the kingdom of darkness, whose king is Satan.

The last book of the Bible reveals where each of these two kings will spend eternity. Revelation 20:10 says, "The Devil who deceived them was thrown into the lake of fire and sulfur where the beast and the false prophet are, and they will be tormented day and night forever and ever."

Revelation 21:1-4 says, "Then I saw a new heaven and a new earth, for the first heaven and the first earth had passed away, and the sea existed no longer. I also saw the Holy City, new Jerusalem, coming down out of heaven from God, prepared as a bride adorned for her husband. Then I heard a loud voice from the throne: Look! God's dwelling is with men, and He will live with them. They will be His people, and God Himself will be with them and be their God. He will wipe away every tear from their eyes.

"Death will exist no longer; grief, crying, and pain will exist no longer, because the previous things have passed away." "And there shall be no more curse: but the throne of God and of the Lamb (Jesus) shall be in it; and his servants shall serve him" (Revelation 22:3).

Your eternal destiny will depend on your decision. It will depend on who you choose to serve, either Jesus or Satan.

Chapter 1 Discussion Questions: The Gospel of the Kingdom

1. What are many of the creatures in the spiritual world around us busy doing?
2. What or who is the focus of this spiritual war?
3. How did this spiritual war start?
4. What was the outcome of Satan's first attack on mankind?
5. What effect did this defeat have on mankind?
6. Was God surprised by Satan's attack and his victory over mankind?
7. How have we all been held in bondage to Satan?
8. What was Satan's plan to win the final victory and have the whole world worship him?

9. How do we know that Satan did not understand God's wisdom and the trap that He set for Satan?
10. How did Jesus defeat Satan?
11. What would be our situation today if God had not raised Jesus from the dead?
12. What two kingdoms are engaged in this spiritual warfare?
13. What effect will it have on someone's eternal destiny whether they serve Jesus or serve Satan?

Obedience to the Gospel

I was having a discussion with a brother recently. He made the statement: "Justification has never, ever, been by faith plus works." I realized that he was probably alluding to Romans 3:20 which states: "By the works of the law no flesh will be justified in His sight."

However, I was a little taken aback as I recalled James 2:24. It says: "You see that a man is justified by works and not by faith alone." This passage obviously contradicts the brother's statement, and apparently, at least according to some, contradicts the passage in Romans 3:20.

A brother once said to me, "If there is an issue that is confusing to me because of *(apparently)* opposing verses, the problem is with my understanding or lack thereof of those verses." I could not agree with him more. If passages of Scripture seem to contradict each other, the problem is not with the Scriptures, the problem is with my understanding of them.

When we come before God and search the Scriptures, it is imperative that we humble ourselves before Him, dropping all of our preconceptions and doctrinal framework that we try to fit Him into, and let Him be God. We need to let Him speak to our hearts and open the eyes of our understanding, that we might see the Scriptures through His eyes and understand according to His heart.

To do this, we must humble ourselves and come before Him with a contrite spirit, with ears to hear and a heart to obey. It is only then that He will begin to reveal the depths of His heart to us, and we will begin to see and understand the mysteries of God hidden in the Scriptures.

James 2:23-24 states: "The Scripture was fulfilled which says, 'And Abraham believed God, and it was reckoned to him as righteousness,' and he was called the friend of God. You see that a man is justified by works and not by faith alone." At first glance, these verses appear to be contradicted by several verses in Romans and Galatians.

Romans 3:28 says: "A man is justified by faith apart from the works of the law." Romans 3:20 assures: "By the works of the law no flesh will be justified in His sight."

Galatians 2:21 observes: "if righteousness comes through the law, then Christ died for nothing." Romans 3:21-22 says: "Apart from the law, God's righteousness has been revealed...that is, God's righteousness through faith in Jesus Christ, to all who believe."

A closer look at these verses reveals that all of the verses cited from Romans and Galatians refer to the law and the works of the law, whereas James refers simply to works. It is obvious from this that James is not referring to the law or the works of the law. James is referring to a different kind of works. We will endeavor to determine what works James is referring to, as these works are apparently essential to be joined with our faith for justification.

John 6:47 says, "I assure you: Anyone who believes has eternal life" (HCSB). It is clear that there is a condition that must be fulfilled for someone to receive eternal life. According to this verse, not everyone receives eternal life, only those who believe. John 3:36 says: "He who believes in the Son has eternal life; but he who does not obey the Son will not see life, but the wrath of God abides on him."

This verse sets out a relationship between believing and obeying. If you believe, you will have the ability, the opportunity to receive eternal life; if you do not obey, you will not see life. To obey refers to something that I have been instructed to do. Either I do what I am instructed to do, such as believe, or I do not obey, and therefore, do not believe.

There are plenty of verses that reinforce this idea. Romans 10:4 says: "For Christ is the end of the law for righteousness to everyone who believes." Romans 10:8-10 announces: "This is the message of faith that we proclaim: If you confess with your mouth, 'Jesus is Lord,' and believe in your heart that God raised Him from the dead, you will be saved. One believes with the heart, resulting in righteousness, and one confesses with the mouth, resulting in salvation" (HCSB).

These verses all talk about conditions that God has placed on our receiving eternal life, righteousness, and salvation. Some of these conditions are that we believe with our heart, and that we confess with our mouth, "Jesus is Lord." The Scriptures tell us that God gives these things to those that obey Him. Acts 5:32 states: "We are witnesses of these things, and so is the Holy Spirit whom God has given to those who obey Him." In Jeremiah 7:23 the Lord says, "Obey me, then I will be your God, and you will be my people" (HCSB).

Peter preaches in Acts 2:36-38 saying: "'Therefore let all the house of Israel know for certain that God has made Him both Lord and Christ—this Jesus whom you crucified.' Now when they heard *this*, they were pierced to the heart, and said to Peter and the rest of the apostles, 'Brethren, what shall we do?' Peter *said* to them, 'Repent, and each of you be baptized in the name of Jesus Christ for the forgiveness of your sins; and you will receive the gift of the Holy Spirit.'" Here God sets forth another condition that must be met in order to be saved. He says we must repent.

The gospel of the kingdom, as set forth in Scripture, declares that by the resurrection of the dead, God has made Jesus to be both Lord and Christ, and thereby, all authority has been given to Him. This gospel tells us that this Jesus is now King of kings and Lord of lords. In fact, in Matthew 28:18-20, Jesus came up and spoke to His disciples proclaiming: "All authority has been given to Me in heaven and on earth. Go therefore and make disciples of all the nations, baptizing them in the name of the Father and the Son and the Holy Spirit, teaching them to observe all that I commanded you."

When this gospel is presented, setting forth Jesus as Lord, showing that all authority has been given unto Him, those hearing this gospel are given an opportunity to decide for themselves, based on the evidence set forth, whether Jesus is who we testify that He is, or not. They can repent, changing their mind about who this Jesus is, and believe in Him, confessing Him as Lord, submitting voluntarily and completely to His authority, or they can choose not to believe and not to submit. They can choose to believe the Son and submit to Him, or they can choose not to believe and not to obey the Son.

Romans 6:16-17 warns: "Don't you know that if you offer yourselves to someone as obedient slaves, you are slaves of that one you obey—either of sin leading to death or of obedience leading to righteousness? But thank God that, although you used to be slaves of sin, you obeyed from the heart that pattern of teaching you were entrusted to" (HCSB). 2 Thessalonians 1:8 tells us God will deal "out retribution to those who do not know God and to those who do not obey the gospel of our Lord Jesus." 1 Peter 4:17 says: "For *it is* time for judgment to begin with the household of God; and if *it begins* with us first, what *will be* the outcome for those who do not obey the gospel of God?"

There are two groups of people in the world today. One group has obeyed the gospel, obeyed the Son, and are doing what is required to meet the conditions set forth by God to receive His gift of eternal life. Those that have responded to the message of faith, the gospel of the kingdom, by doing works of obedience, such as repenting, believing, confessing, submitting the Lordship of Jesus Christ, have been quali-fied to receive the gift of God, the inheritance of eternal life (Colossians 1:12). Their works of obedience added to, or joined with, their faith results in righteousness, justification, and salvation.

Those that have refused to obey the gospel, who have refused to obey the Son, will not see life. They will receive retribution from God and will fall under His judgment. Their end will be in the lake of fire. Revelation 20:14-15 reveals: "Death and Hades were thrown into the lake of fire. This is the second death, the lake of fire. And anyone not found written in the book of life was thrown into the lake of fire."

All of these passages are about eternal life, salvation, righteousness, and justification. They all demonstrate that these things are freely given by God. These things cannot be earned by the works of the law, or by good works. These passages do, however, make it very clear that God only gives these things to those who have met the conditions that He has set. He only gives these things to those who obey the gospel message, to those who obey the Son by believing the testimony of the gospel of the kingdom and by submitting to His authority, confessing "Jesus is Lord."

I have heard some say, "Everything has been done. There is nothing that you need to do. When Jesus died on the cross he cried out, 'It is finished.' He has done everything, and there is nothing that you need to do." That, however, was not Peter's response in Acts 2:38.

When the people asked what they must do, Peter did not tell them, "Everything has been done. Jesus did it all. There is nothing left for you to do." No, rather, Peter said: "Repent, and be baptized, each of you, in the name of Jesus Christ for the forgiveness of your sins, and you will receive the gift of the Holy Spirit."

Yes, Jesus did it all. He paid the full price required by God. He completed the work of atonement and redemption. During His life, and in His death on the cross, Jesus fulfilled every righteous requirement of God for our justification. However, Peter realized, that even though Jesus had finished His work, there remained something that those who heard the gospel message still had to do to be saved.

Peter gave them specific instructions as to what was expected of them, of what they had to do to be saved. Those that obeyed were added to the church that day. Those that accepted his message did works of obedience that, added to their faith, resulted in justification and the promise of eternal life.

According to *Strong's Exhaustive Concordance* the word "obey" in Acts 5:32 means to be persuaded by a ruler, to submit to authority. The word "believe" means to entrust to, to have faith in, to commit to. The word "faith" means a conviction or assurance.

When we have faith in Jesus, we have been persuaded that He is who Scripture declares Him to be. This faith must be joined together with works of obedience, such as repenting, submitting to, confessing, and believing. We are then justified by works and not by faith alone. Again, these works are not works of the law, or good works, but are works of obedience in response to the gospel message of Jesus and the Kingdom of God.

James 2:19 affirms: "the demons also believe, and shudder." However, the demons do not join their knowledge of who Jesus is with works of obedience. They do not freely submit to His authority. May we encourage all of the people that we share the gospel with that there are works of obedience that they need to do that will result in righteousness, salvation, and eternal life.

Does everyone have eternal life? No! John 3:36 says, "He who believes in the Son has eternal life; but he who does not obey the Son will not see life, but the wrath of God abides on him." In order to receive eternal life, there is a condition that we have to meet. There is something we have to do. We must obey the Son.

Only he who "believes in the Son" has eternal life. There are works of obedience that must be joined to our faith in order for us to be justified. Justification always requires faith plus works of obedience. It requires that we respond to the gospel message by believing and submitting to Jesus as Lord!

John 6:26-29 tells us, "Jesus answered them and said, 'Truly, truly, I say to you, you seek Me, not because you saw signs, but because you ate of the loaves and were filled. Do not work for the food which perishes, but for the food which endures to eternal life, which the Son of Man will give you, for on Him the Father, God, has set His seal.' Therefore they said to Him, 'What shall we do, so that we may work the works of God?' Jesus answered and said to them, 'This is the work of God, that you believe in Him whom He has sent.'"

Believing is the work "for the food which endures to eternal life." To believe is to obey the Son. The one who believes the Son has the promise of inheriting eternal life. The one who does not obey the Son will not see life, but the wrath of God abides on him.

Let us look again at James 2:23-24. It says, "And Abraham believed God, and it was reckoned to him as righteousness." This passage is given to us by James as proof that "a man is justified by works and not by faith alone." What works is James referring to? It says Abraham believed God. The only thing here that Abraham is said to have done is to believe. He believed. That is the work that justified him. This is the work of God, that you believe in Him whom He has sent.

Man is justified by works and not by faith alone. There are works that God requires us to do to be justified. These works of obedience must be joined with our faith.

God has made promises of reward to those that by faith believe His word and obey. He has also made promises of wrath and retribution to those that rebel and refuse to obey. When we proclaim this gospel of the kingdom, may we be faithful to encourage our hearers that there is something that they must do in response to the gospel message in order to be saved. They must obey God and continue in obedience that they may inherit all the promises of the gospel of the kingdom.

Chapter 2 Discussion Questions:
Obedience to the Gospel

1. What does James 2:23-24 say about justification?
2. What does Romans 3:28 say about justification?
3. Who has eternal life?
4. Who will not see life?
5. What is the message of faith in Romans 10:8-10?
6. What is the gospel of the kingdom as set forth in Scripture?
7. How do you know whose slave you will be?
8. What are the two groups of people in the world today?
9. How did Jesus complete His work of atonement and redemption?
10. What remains for those that hear the gospel message to do?
11. Does everyone have eternal life?
12. What did Jesus say is the work of God?
13. What work did Abraham do that justified him?

Receiving the Promises

A little more than three years ago, I began to seek the Lord again for direction in my life. I made a request for prayer concerning this matter. That evening, the Lord opened my eyes to see four twenty-nines. It was four different passages that contained verse twenty-nine.

The first passage was Matthew 19:29. It says, "And everyone who has left houses or brothers or sisters or father or mother or children or farms for My name's sake, will receive many times as much, and will inherit eternal life." The next passage was Mark 10:29-30. It says, Jesus said, "Truly I say to you, there is no one who has left house or brothers or sisters or mother or father or children or farms, for My sake and for the gospel's sake, but that he will receive a hundred times as much now in the present age, houses and brothers and sisters and mothers and children and farms, along with persecutions; and in the age to come, eternal life."

The third passage was Luke 18:29. It says, "And He said to them, 'Truly I say to you, there is no one who has left house or wife or brothers or parents or children, for the sake of the kingdom of God, who will not receive many times as much at this time and in the age to come, eternal life.'" The last passage was 1 Corinthians 7:29-31. It says, "But this I say, brethren, the time has been shortened, so that from now on those who have wives should be as though they had none; and those who weep, as though they did not weep; and those who rejoice, as though they did not rejoice; and those who buy, as though they did not possess; and those who use the world, as though they did not make full use of it; for the form of this world is passing away."

These passages began to convince me that the time is short, and we need to be about the Lord's business. The Lord Jesus must have the preeminence in our lives. We must be so passionately in love with Him that nothing else matters as much as living to please Him.

He then brought me to Matthew 7:21-24. It says, "Not everyone who says to Me, 'Lord, Lord,' will enter the kingdom of heaven, but he who does the will of My Father who is in heaven will enter. Many will say to Me on that day, 'Lord, Lord, did we not prophesy in Your name, and in Your name cast out demons, and in Your name perform many miracles?' And then I will declare to them, 'I never knew you; DEPART FROM ME, YOU WHO PRACTICE LAWLESSNESS.' Therefore everyone who hears these words of Mine and acts on them, may be compared to a wise man who built his house on the rock."

From this passage, it became evident that the Lord does not want us to do great things for Him. He is only interested in our listening, that we would hear His words, and that we would act in obedience to the words that He speaks to us. It is essential that we have ears to hear and a heart to obey. It does not matter what great thing we do for the Lord, if it is not out of obedience to His speaking, it is lawlessness.

My first thought was, wow, that sounds harsh. However, the Lord began to remind me of how much He loves us, that He freely laid down His life for us. He wants us to understand that He has prepared only the best for us, but the only way we can begin to receive it and enjoy it is by obeying Him. We enter into all of the blessings, all of the promises that He has prepared for us only by being persuaded of His love and His goodness toward us and by obeying Him.

When God begins to reveal to us who Jesus is, He commands us to believe on Him, to allow ourselves to be persuaded by the evidence of who Jesus is. As we yield ourselves to His speaking, and begin to believe in Jesus, we find ourselves starting to think differently about Jesus and about how we have been living. We begin to repent.

As we repent, we begin to confess what we have come to realize in our heart about Jesus, that He truly is Lord of all. As we repent, and believe, and confess Jesus as Lord, we begin to realize something amazing is happening. It is like we are being born all over again, only this time we are not being born into a physical material world, but into a spiritual one. We begin the incredible experience of realizing that we have been transferred from death into life, from darkness into light. We begin to experience all the fear that we have lived with for our entire lives vanishing away, being washed away by floods of love, and joy, and peace, peace that surpasses all understanding.

We begin to realize how much Christ suffered, how much He endured so that we would be able to be restored to fellowship with Him and with His Father in heaven. We just begin to scratch the surface of the depths of the love that God has for us in Christ Jesus our Lord. Simply obeying His command to believe resulted in the indescribable blessing of being born again and receiving the Holy Spirit into our spirit, making our spirit alive and restoring us to fellowship with God who is spirit. How much more does He have in store for us if we would continue to listen to His speaking and continue to obey Him?

We cannot even begin to imagine the blessings that He has prepared for us as He begins the process of sanctification in our lives, of setting us apart from the world unto Himself. We soon find that our slightest obedience is richly rewarded by receiving more of His promises, both now and in the age to come, as the life-giving Spirit begins to teach us all that is ours in Christ (1 Corinthians 2:12).

I soon began to realize from these four passages the many blessings that He promised. Many blessings for this life and many others are for the next age. I began to consider which of the promises I could expect to receive in this life and which of the promises would have to wait. It occurred to me that it was important to know which promises I should expect to be fulfilled in this life and which I should not. Unrealized expectations can result in frustration and disappointment. God does not want us to be frustrated and disappointed. He wants us to know and understand His will, that our expectations would be according to His word and His will.

In these four passages and in Matthew 5, we see many things mentioned that we can expect to experience in this life. When we leave families, houses, and farms, we will receive many times more in this life. We will mourn, be persecuted, and suffer many things, but God, by His Spirit working within us will use these things help us grow to maturity. These things will help to make us poor in spirit, meek, hungry and thirsty for righteousness, merciful, pure in heart and peacemakers. As we walk by the Spirit, Galatians 5:22-23 assures us that we will bear fruit of love, joy, peace, patience, kindness, goodness, faith, gentleness, and self-control.

If we faithfully obey, being led by the indwelling Holy Spirit, we can expect many blessings in the age to come. We will inherit the kingdom of heaven, we will inherit the earth, we will inherit eternal life. We will be comforted, satisfied, receive mercy, and be called the sons of God. According to Revelation 21:1-7, there will be no more sorrow, crying, or tears, and death will be no longer. All of these things will be the inheritance of the faithful, overcoming believers.

In just the past few months, it has dawned on me that the four twenty-nines all speak of eternal life as being an inheritance that we will receive in the next age. This understanding was contrary to everything that I had been taught and come to believe about eternal life over the last forty years. I was troubled by this contradiction and I began to seek the Lord for clarification.

I was reminded that, if there is an apparent contradiction between various passages of Scripture, there must be something wrong with my understanding of one or more of those passages. As I reviewed several passages that spoke about receiving eternal life, I began to examine the meaning of some of the Greek words used in those passages.

One of these verses is John 3:36 which says, "He who believes in the Son has eternal life; but he who does not obey the Son will not see life, but the wrath of God abides on him." Another is John 6:47 which says, "Truly, truly, I say to you, he who believes has eternal life."

The word "has" in these verses is translated from the Greek word "echo" meaning "to hold," referring to holding the ability to have something, or the conditions of holding on to something. It refers to something that you have the ability to receive if the required conditions are met. It also means that if the conditions are not met, you will lose the opportunity to receive that which was promised.

It is reminiscent of John 1:12 which says, "But as many as received Him, to them He gave the right (the privilege or opportunity) to become children of God, even to those who believe in His name." With this new understanding of these verses, there is no longer any contradiction with the verses that say that eternal life is an inheritance that we will receive in the age to come.

We are told in Revelation 2:7 that the victor, the faithful overcoming believer, will have the right to eat of the tree of life. We last saw the tree of life in Genesis 2 and 3. Except for a few verses in the book of Proverbs, we do not see the tree of life again in Scripture until in the book Revelation, in the New Jerusalem, on the new earth.

In Genesis 3, the way to the tree of life was blocked until man's problem of sin was fully dealt with. The final stroke in dealing with sin in a believer's life takes place with the death of his physical body of flesh. Romans 7:18-20 says, "For I know that nothing good dwells in me, that is, in my flesh; for the willing is present in me, but the doing of the good is not. For the good that I want to do, I do not do, but I practice the very evil that I do not want. But if I am doing the very thing I do not want, I am no longer the one doing it, but sin which dwells in me." The thing that is not good that dwells in our flesh is sin. The sin in our flesh is eliminated by the removal of the body of flesh through death.

Paul goes on to tell us in Romans 8:18-25, "For I consider that the sufferings of this present time are not worthy to be compared with the glory that is to be revealed to us. For...creation waits eagerly for the revealing of the sons of God. . . in hope that the creation itself also will be set free from its slavery to corruption...the whole creation groans...And not only this, but we also ourselves, having the first fruits of the Spirit, even we ourselves groan within ourselves, waiting eagerly for our adoption as sons, the redemption of our body. For in hope we have been saved, but hope that is seen is not hope; for who hopes for what he already sees? But if we hope for what we do not see, with perseverance we wait eagerly for it." Titus 1:2 and 3:7 both speak of the "hope of eternal life" which God promised long ages ago.

We groan within ourselves, eagerly waiting for the adoption, the redemption of our bodies. Creation eagerly waits for the sons of God to be revealed, that creation itself would be set free from the bondage of corruption. We wait eagerly to receive the promise, the inheritance of the saints, the adoption as sons, when we will be called the sons of God, when He will dwell with us and we will be His sons. We hope for this eternal life, because we have not yet received it.

Paul writes about this in 1 Corinthians 15:50-53, "Now I say this, brethren, that flesh and blood cannot inherit the kingdom of God; nor does the perishable inherit the imperishable. Behold, I tell you a mystery; we will not all sleep, but we will all be changed, in a moment, in the twinkling of an eye, at the last trumpet; for the trumpet will sound, and the dead will be raised imperishable, and we will be changed. For this perishable must put on the imperishable, and this mortal must put on immortality." We will all be changed. In a moment, in the twinkling of an eye, at the last trumpet, the dead will be raised incorruptible and we will be changed.

Born-again believers now, in this life, have the full promises of God restored to them. They now have the opportunity, through faithful obedience, to receive all of God's promises, including eternal life. The believer is back to a situation very similar to that of Adam in the garden of Eden.

Adam had two sources of life that he could choose to live by. He could choose to live by the fruit of the tree of the knowledge of good and evil, or he could choose to live by the fruit of the tree of life.

One, the tree of the knowledge of good and evil, where God is disrespected and disobeyed, where man is enabled to live in whatever way seems right to him, the end of which is death. The other, the tree of life, where God is believed and trusted as one that is good and wants the best for man, the end of which is eternal life.

The born-again believer has now a similar situation. He has two natures, two different sources according to which he can choose to live. He can choose to live according to the flesh, or he can choose to live according to the Spirit.

He is no longer a slave to sin, under sin's control and domination. He can however choose to disrespect God and disobey God and live according to the lustful desires of the flesh, which leads to death. Or he can choose to believe God, trusting and honoring God as one that is good and desires and promises to provide only the best for man. The believer does this by living a life in humble obedience to the indwelling Holy Spirit, resulting in sanctification, the end of which is eternal life (Romans 6:22).

When we are born again, we obtain an inheritance. Ephesians 1:11 says, "We have obtained an inheritance, having been predestined according to His purpose who works all things after the counsel of His will." He has given the ability through the empowering of the indwelling Holy Spirit to eventually, if we endure to the end, receive the inheritance that has been promised to the faithful, to the victor.

When we were born again, God qualified us by placing us into Christ to receive the inheritance among the saints. Colossians 1:12 says, "Giving thanks to the Father, who has qualified us to share in the inheritance of the saints in Light." Colossians 3:24 says, "From the Lord you will receive the reward of the inheritance." Through the adoption as sons, we are changed. We, the faithful believers, put on immortality and receive eternal life.

Hebrews 12:17 says of Esau who sold his birthright, "For you know that even afterwards, when he desired to inherit the blessing, he was rejected, for he found no place for repentance, though he sought for it with tears." May none of us be like Esau who failed to understand the significance of his birthright and therefore did not value it as something extremely precious. Instead, he sold his birthright for a bowl of stew.

Eternal life is the birthright of every born-again believer. May we reflect on how precious this birthright of ours really is. May we value it above all else. Jesus tells us in John 17:3, "This is eternal life, that they may know You, the only true God, and Jesus Christ whom You have sent." Eternal life means living continually in the presence of God and of the Lamb in the New Jerusalem, on the new earth, knowing Him, seeing Him face to face, serving Him, eating of the tree of life, and enjoying the fullness of all the promises we have inherited through faithful obedience to Him.

This is exactly what Paul was talking about in Philippians 3:8 where he says, "I count all things to be loss in view of the surpassing value of knowing Christ Jesus my Lord, for whom I have suffered the loss of all things, and count them but rubbish so that I may gain Christ." Again, in verse 10 Paul says, "That I may know Him and the power of His resurrection and the fellowship of His sufferings, being conformed to His death; in order that I may attain to the resurrection from the dead."

Paul writes in I Corinthians 13, "For now we see only a reflection as in a mirror; then we shall see face to face. Now I know in part; then I shall know fully, even as I am fully known." When Jesus returns, we shall see Him face to face. When He returns, and the veil of our flesh is removed, we shall know Him as fully as we are known.

1 Peter 3:9 says, "You were called for the very purpose that you might inherit a blessing." Is there any greater blessing than this, that we may know Him, that we might inherit eternal life? This is the purpose for which we have been called.

1 Peter 1:3-4 says, "Blessed be the God and Father of our Lord Jesus Christ, who according to His great mercy has caused us to be born again to a living hope through the resurrection of Jesus Christ from the dead, to obtain an inheritance which is imperishable and undefiled and will not fade away, reserved in heaven for you."

Matthew 25:34 says, "Then the King will say to those on His right, 'Come, you who are blessed of My Father, inherit the kingdom prepared for you from the foundation of the world.'" 1 John 2:25 says, "As for you, let that abide in you which you heard from the beginning. If what you heard from the beginning abides in you, you also will abide in the Son and in the Father. This is the promise which He Himself made to us: eternal life."

In order to receive the inheritance with the saints in light, there is a condition that we have to meet. There is something that we have to do. We must continue to faithfully "obey the Son." This is not just a one-time obedience. To receive the inheritance, we must remain faithful and endure to the end. Only the faithful, only the victorious, will receive the inheritance of all the blessings that God has prepared for us.

We have been saved by believing, by obeying. We will be saved if we continue to believe and obey. If we continue faithful until the end, we will inherit eternal life, we will inherit all the promises of God.

Chapter 3 Discussion Questions: Receiving the Promises

1. What are the four twenty-nines?
2. According to these passages, when will we receive eternal life?
3. Why did Jesus not accept those in Matthew 7 that said, "Lord, Lord?"
4. To gain entrance into the kingdom of heaven, what does Jesus say we must do?
5. Why does the Lord require obedience?
6. How do we know that God loves us?
7. What is the indescribably great blessing that we received as a result of believing Jesus?
8. What are some of the blessings that God promises to give us in this life?
9. What are some of the blessings that God promises to give us in the next life?
10. What is the meaning of the Greek word "echo?"
11. When will the faithful, overcoming believers eat of the tree of life and live forever?
12. What are we and all of creation eagerly waiting for?

13. How is the born-again believer's situation similar to that of Adam?

14. What does Ephesians 1:11 and Colossians 1:12 say concerning the inheritance?

15. What is the birthright of every born-again believer?

16. What did Paul state as his goal in Philippians 3?

17. What does 1 Peter 3:9 say is the purpose of our having been called by God?

18. What must we do to receive the inheritance that God has prepared for us?

Full Salvation

"Seek the Lord while He may still be found"
(Isaiah 55:6).

R omans 1:16-21 says, "For I am not ashamed of the Good News of Christ, for it is the power of God for salvation for everyone who believes, for the Jew first, and also for the Greek. For in it is revealed God's righteousness from faith to faith. As it is written, "The righteous shall live by faith.

"For the wrath of God is revealed from heaven against all ungodliness and unrighteousness of men who suppress the truth in unrighteousness, because that which is known of God is revealed in them, for God revealed it to them. For the invisible things of him since the creation of the world are clearly seen, being perceived through the things that are made, even his everlasting power and divinity, that they may be without excuse. Because knowing God, they didn't glorify him as God, and didn't give thanks, but became vain in their reasoning, and their senseless heart was darkened." (WEB).

I encourage you to observe creation and behold the testimony of God. According to this passage in Romans 1, God has revealed His power and divinity through creation, through the things that have been made. Through his creation God also reveals his wrath against all ungodliness and unrighteousness.

God reveals even more of Himself through the good news, the gospel of Jesus Christ. In this good news of Christ, we see God's righteousness revealed. In it we see God in all His greatness, goodness and love.

God is continually revealing Himself to all of us, so that all will be without excuse. From the testimony of creation, from the testimony of the Scriptures, we all know God, we all know He exists. However, knowing God, we do not glorify Him as God, neither are we thankful for all that He has provided for us. Instead we vainly reason that we have the things we have because we earned them, because we deserved them.

Search the Scriptures and listen to the testimony of God and His full, loving provision for you in Jesus Christ. John 3:16 says, "For God so loved the world, that he gave his one and only Son, that whoever believes in him should not perish, but have eternal life" (WEB).

John 3:36 says, "One who believes in the Son has eternal life, but one who disobeys the Son won't see life, but the wrath of God remains on him" (WEB). John 20:31 says, "These things are written, that you may believe that Jesus is the Christ, the Son of God, and that believing you may have life in his name" (WEB). Thoughtfully weigh all of the evidence of creation and of Scripture and determine for yourself, once and for all, who this Jesus really is.

As you observe creation, notice the incredible vastness of the universe. Also notice the minute, intricate details, the amazing colors and smells of the diverse array of flowers and plants growing all around you. Observe the birds, the insects, and the animals. The beauty and the order of creation are breathtakingly majestic. Creation in its majesty demands that there must be a creator with a master design.

Whenever I admire any building, whether it is a simple house or an enormous skyscraper, I am brought to the realization that someone designed it, that someone built it. There is no doubt in my mind that the building did not just come into being on its own. I am positive that the building was not the result of some random explosion. No matter how much time might have been allowed to elapse, it could not build itself out of nothing. Simple logic, and a little experience, assures me that someone had to have designed it and someone had to have built it.

How much more does logic and experience teach us that the origin of the universe, and of all creation as we know it, was not by accident? No matter how many people, and how many books, have told us otherwise, deep in our hearts, after thoughtful consideration, we are compelled to admit that there is a God of creation.

The next question is whether we are going to acknowledge God as God. Romans 1:18-20 says, "For the wrath of God is revealed from heaven against all ungodliness and unrighteousness of men who suppress the truth in unrighteousness, because that which is known about God is evident within them; because God made it evident to them. For since the creation of the world His invisible attributes, His eternal power and divine nature, having been clearly seen, being understood through what has been made, so that they are without excuse."

Immediately, we realize, if we acknowledge Him as God, there is going to be a requirement that we will be held accountable to His standards for how we live. It is obvious that He is a God of order, and therefore, He will expect us to live orderly lives in compliance with His standards. Romans 3:19 reaffirms this, "Now we know that whatever the Law says, it speaks to those who are under the Law, so that every mouth may be closed and all the world may be accountable to God."

This realization is alarming because, if we are honest with ourselves, we have to admit that we do not have the strength or the ability within ourselves to live up to the standards set by a holy God. Romans 3:20 warns us, "By the works of the Law no flesh will be justified in His sight." With this realization, our sense of hopelessness is met with despair, until we read in the Scriptures that, while we were still sinners, God sent His only Son to die for us, to die in our place. Romans 5:6 tells us, "For while we were still helpless, at the right time Christ died for the ungodly." Romans 5:8 continues, "God demonstrates His own love toward us, in that while we were yet sinners, Christ died for us."

We also learn from the Scriptures that God's Son, Jesus, not only died for us, but was also raised up from the dead to live in us. 1 Peter 3:18 says, "For Christ also died for sins once for all, the just for the unjust, so that He might bring us to God, having been put to death in the flesh, but made alive in the spirit." 1 John 3:24 says, "The one who keeps His commandments abides in Him, and He in him. We know by this that He abides in us, by the Spirit whom He has given us."

By His resurrection, Jesus broke the power of death over us. Hebrews 2:14 tells us, "Since the children share in flesh and blood, He Himself likewise also partook of the same, that through death He might render powerless him who had the power of death, that is, the devil, and might free those who through fear of death were subject to slavery all their lives." We find that if we submit to Jesus as Lord, He will deliver us from the penalty of sin, which is death, by forgiving our sins.

Here we come to a crossroads. Now we need to make a decision. This decision must not be made based on emotions. It must be made, as a juror in a courtroom, based only on the evidence that has been presented. We need to take some time to consider all of the evidence.

Who is this Jesus? Is He the Son of God? Did God raise Him up from the dead never to die again? Did God, by the power of the resurrection make Him to be both Lord and Christ?

Acts 2:32 proclaims, "This Jesus God raised up again, to which we are all witnesses." Acts 2:36 declares, "Therefore let all the house of Israel know for certain that God has made Him both Lord and Christ–this Jesus whom you crucified."

If you allow yourself to be persuaded by the facts, by the evidence presented, and you believe that God raised

Jesus from the dead, that results in righteousness. You need to simply declare what you now believe. You need to confess with your mouth "Jesus is Lord" resulting in salvation (Romans 10:9-10). The Spirit of Christ coming to indwell your spirit is the beginning of the salvation process. This can only happen by genuine faith in Jesus.

Ephesians 2:4-5 says: "But God, being rich in mercy, because of His great love with which He loved us, even when we were dead in our transgressions, made us alive together with Christ (by grace you have been saved)." Paul says here that we have been saved, if we were made alive with Christ by His life indwelling us as the Spirit within our spirit. If God quickened us, made us alive, by placing the Spirit of Christ within our spirit, then we have been saved. This is the salvation of our spirit.

Paul also writes to the believers in Rome: "For if while we were enemies we were reconciled to God through the death of His Son, much more, having been reconciled, we shall be saved by His life" (Romans 5:10). We find that Christ, by the power of His life within us, has also set us free from the control and dominance of sin in our lives.

Romans 6:5-11 says, "For if we have become united with Him in the likeness of His death, certainly we shall also be in the likeness of His resurrection, knowing this, that our old self was crucified with Him, in order that our body of sin might be done away with, so that we would no longer be slaves to sin; for he who has died is freed from sin. Now if we have died with Christ, we believe that we shall also live with Him, knowing that Christ, having been raised from the dead, is never to die again; death no longer is master over Him. For the death that He died, He died to sin once for all; but the life that He lives, He lives to God. Even so consider yourselves to be dead to sin."

Romans 8:2 says, "For the law of the Spirit of life in Christ Jesus has set you free from the law of sin and of death." We no longer need to obey sin and be held in bondage to it. Christ has given us full salvation from sin by the power of His Holy Spirit indwelling our human spirit. When God formed man, He formed the spirit of man within him.

Zachariah 12:1 says, "Thus declares the Lord who stretches out the heavens, lays the foundation of the earth, and forms the spirit of man within him." Jesus says in John 3:6, "That which is born of the flesh is flesh, and that which is born of the Spirit is spirit." When the Holy Spirit comes to indwell us we are born again, our spirit is born of the Spirit of God.

We understand that our spirit was made alive when we were saved, by being born again. But now, much more than that, we shall be saved, by the power of His life working within us to transform our soul, to conform us to His very image. This is yet another aspect of salvation, the salvation of our soul.

Eventually we learn, through the teaching and guidance of His indwelling Spirit, that by His divine nature, He has given us everything we need to live lives pleasing to God. 1 Corinthians 2:12 reminds us, "Now we have received, not the spirit of the world, but the Spirit who is from God, so that we may know the things freely given to us by God." 2 Peter 1:3 encourages us saying, "His divine power has granted to us everything pertaining to life and godliness, through the true knowledge of Him who called us by His own glory and excellence." Christ, by His Spirit, empowers us to do everything that God might require of us.

Paul tells us in Philippians 4:13, "I can do all things through Christ who strengthens me." We find that we have been transferred from a life of darkness and despair, into a life of love, joy, and peace in the Holy Spirit. Colossians 1:13-14 says, "For He rescued us from the domain of darkness, and transferred us to the kingdom of His beloved Son." Galatians 5:22-23 continues, "The fruit of the Spirit is love, joy, peace, patience, kindness, goodness, faithfulness, gentleness, self- control; against such things there is no law."

We begin to experience, more and more, that the love, joy, and peace in the Spirit is now gradually spreading out from our spirit into our very soul by the power of His indestructible life working within us. As we walk by the Spirit, in joyful submission to Jesus as our Lord, we continue to experience the gradual process of our soul being transformed into the image of Christ, as our mind is being renewed day by day. Romans 12:2 instructs us, "Do not be conformed to the world, but be transformed by the renewing of your mind, so that you may prove what the will of God is, that which is good and acceptable and perfect." 2 Corinthians 4:16 encourages us, "Therefore we do not lose heart, but though our outer man is decaying, yet our inner man is being renewed day by day." This is the salvation of our soul.

We even begin to understand the promise of Scripture, that "if the Spirit of him who raised Jesus from the dead is living in you, he who raised Christ from the dead will also give life to your mortal bodies because of his Spirit who lives in you" (Romans 8:11, NIV). This refers to what Paul spoke of in 1 Corinthians 15:51-52: "Behold, I tell you a mystery; we will not all sleep, but we will all be changed, in a moment, in the twinkling of an eye, at the last trumpet; for the trumpet will sound, and the dead will be raised imperishable, and we will be changed." We see yet another aspect of salvation. This refers to the salvation of our bodies.

As believers, we were saved when we were born again, when the Spirit of Christ made our spirit alive. We are being saved day by day as the life of Christ within us transforms our soul into His image. We will be saved when our body is transfigured at the last trumpet sound, when in a twinkling of an eye we are changed. This corresponds to Paul's prayer in 1 Thessalonians 5:23: "Now may the God of peace Himself sanctify you entirely; and may your spirit and soul and body be preserved complete, without blame at the coming of our Lord Jesus Christ." Our spirit has been saved, our soul is being saved, and our body will be saved. This is truly a full salvation.

Now, as born-again believers, we learn that we no longer need to fear the "second death." Revelation 2:11 comforts us saying, "He who has an ear, let him hear what the Spirit says to the churches. He who overcomes will not be hurt by the second death." Now we only need to be concerned about the coming judgment from the standpoint of being held accountable for our works, whether good or bad.

2 Corinthians 5:10 reminds us, "For we must all appear before the judgment seat of Christ, so that each one may be recompensed for his deeds in the body, according to what he has done, whether good of bad." Now, as genuine believers, our only concern is whether we will be found to have walked by the Spirit in obedience to God, or whether we continued to live according to the desires of the flesh. That is what believers will be judged on.

Paul refers to this judgment in 1 Corinthians 3:7-15 where he writes: "So then neither the one who plants nor the one who waters is anything, but only God who gives the growth. Now the one planting and the one watering are one in purpose, and each will receive his own reward according to his own labor. For we are God's co-workers. You are God's field, God's building. According to God's grace that was given to me, I have laid a foundation as a skilled master builder, and another builds on it. But each one must be careful how he builds on it. For no one can lay any other foundation than what has been laid down. That foundation is Jesus Christ.

"If anyone builds on that foundation with gold, silver, costly stones, wood, hay, or straw, each one's work will become obvious, for the day will disclose it, because it will be revealed by fire; the fire will test the quality of each one's work. If anyone's work that he has built survives, he will receive a reward. If anyone's work is burned up, it will be lost, but he will be saved; yet it will be like an escape through fire." Here we see a judgment of believers, with a reward or loss, based on our works. This judgment is based on whether our works were done in obedience to the Lord, according to His empowering, or whether our works were according to our own understanding, by our own strength.

Hebrews 10:30-31 warns, "The Lord will judge His people. It is a terrifying thing to fall into the hands of the living God!" In 2 Corinthians 5:9-10 Paul writes to the Christians, the believers, in Corinth saying: "It is our aim, therefore, to please him, whether we are 'at home' or 'away'" (Phillips).

There are some that say that Christians do not have to worry about the judgment. They say that the judgment is only for unbelievers. It is clear from these passages that Scripture does not support that teaching. In fact, the teaching that believers will not be judged leads those that believe it into a careless and often godless lifestyle.

The passage we looked at above from 1 Corinthians 3:7-15 makes it very clear that Christians will indeed be judged according to their works. If their works are of the flesh, and not of the Spirit, they will suffer loss, their works will be burned up, though they themselves will be saved as through fire. The greater danger is that believers that live careless lives, not walking by the Spirit, will forever miss out on the opportunity to gain as much of Christ as they otherwise might have.

1 Corinthians 15:41-42 says: "There is one glory of the sun, and another glory of the moon, and another glory of the stars; for star differs from star in glory. So also is the resurrection of the dead." The glory that each believer shall have in the resurrection shall differ from one another based on the amount of Christ they had allowed to fill their soul during their lifetime, not based on who they were or what they had accomplished. Paul prays for the believers in Ephesians 3:19: "that you may be filled up to all the fullness of God."

Paul declares in Philippians 3:8-9, "I count all things to be loss in view of the surpassing value of knowing Christ Jesus my Lord, for whom I have suffered the loss of all things, and count them but rubbish so that I may gain Christ, and may be found in Him, not having a righteousness of my own derived from *the* Law, but that which is through faith in Christ, the righteousness which *comes* from God on the basis of faith." Paul again says, "But we should always give thanks to God for you, brethren beloved by the Lord, because God has chosen you from the beginning for salvation through sanctification by the Spirit and faith in the truth. It was for this He called you through our gospel, that you may gain the glory of our Lord Jesus Christ" (2 Thessalonians 2:13-14).

Do not be deceived. Scripture is very clear about this point. We will all have to give account to God for the things we do. We will all have to give account for how we live. In Romans 14:10 Paul writes to the believers in Rome reminding them that "we will all stand before the judgment seat of God." He continues in verse twelve saying, "So then each one of us will give an account of himself to God."

"And just as surely as it is appointed for all men to die and after that pass to their judgment, so it is certain that Christ was offered once to bear the sins of many and after that, to those who look for him, he will appear a second time, not this time to deal with sin, but to bring them to full salvation" (Hebrews 9:28). Do not miss out on all that God has prepared for those that love Him (1 Corinthians 2:9).

Chapter 4 Discussion Questions:
Full Salvation

1. In what ways does God reveal Himself to mankind?
2. How does God demonstrate His love toward us?
3. Why did Christ die for our sins?
4. How do we go about deciding who this Jesus is?
5. What is the message of faith presented in Romans 10:9-10?

6. What is the salvation of our spirit?
7. What is the salvation of our soul?
8. What is the salvation of our bodies?
9. How will believers be judged when they stand before the judgment seat of Christ?
10. When Christ appears a second time, what will be His purpose for those who look for Him?

Assurance of Salvation

A s we have already seen, the gospel found in Scripture is the gospel of the kingdom. This word "gospel" means good news. The gospel of the kingdom is the good news of the kingdom God established when He gave all authority unto Jesus, raising Him from the dead, making Him both Lord and Christ (Acts 2:32-36).

By raising Him from the dead, never to die again (Romans 6:9) so that He would never undergo decay (Acts 2:27), God declared Him to be the Son of God (Romans 1:4), the very God Himself (John 10:31-36). It is by believing in our heart that God raised Jesus from the dead, resulting in righteousness, and confessing with our mouth, Jesus as Lord, resulting in salvation, that we are able to enter into this kingdom of God (Romans 10:9-10, Colossians 1:13-14).

It is only as we repent, as we change our mind about Jesus and joyfully submit to Him, believing and confessing Him as Lord, that we are ushered into this kingdom and are born of the Spirit, receiving the forgiveness of sins and the gift of the Holy Spirit (Acts 2:38).

We then begin a life-long experience of entering into the fullness of the riches of Christ Jesus our Lord, the King of this magnificent kingdom of light. In Acts 26:18, the Lord tells Paul that he was sending him to the Gentiles "to open their eyes so that they may turn from darkness to light and from the dominion of Satan to God, that they may receive forgiveness of sins and an inheritance among those who have been sanctified by faith in Me."

By the death and resurrection of Jesus, the Christ, the power of Satan was broken, and we were set free from his dominion, free from the dominion of sin, set free to serve God in the obedience that results in righteousness. Romans 6:6 tells us, "For we know that our old self was crucified with Him in order that sin's dominion over the body might be abolished, so that we may no longer be enslaved to sin" (HCSB). Romans 6:12 continues, "Therefore do not let sin reign in your mortal body, so that you obey its lusts."

Paul says in Galatians 1:7 that there are some that distort the gospel of Christ. He says in Galatians 1:9 that "if any man is preaching to you a gospel contrary to that which you received, let him be accursed." You can see that in God's eyes, it is not a small thing to preach another gospel. Anyone that does is an enemy of the gospel. Jesus said clearly, "He who is not with me is against me" (Matthew 12:30).

There is another gospel that is being preached today. It has become very popular with some pastors and with some evangelists. It is called the gospel of repentance. It is a gospel without cost or discomfort. It is "another gospel." The focus of this gospel is the sinner and their sins. The focus is not on the kingdom of God and Jesus Christ as Lord.

This gospel teaches people that God has a law that must be kept, and that it is sin to break that law. It teaches that all have sinned and that the wages of sin is death. It teaches that if they do not repent of their sins, feeling sorry for them and ask Jesus to come into their heart and be their savior, they are going to spend eternity in the torment of unquenchable fire. If they do repent (feel sorry), and ask Jesus into their heart, then they will be saved and will go to heaven when they die.

Then, after sufficient manipulation of the emotions through the use of stories and music, they ask how many would like to be saved and know for sure they are going to heaven when they die. Then they ask the people to raise their hand or come down front or say the sinner's prayer with them. After doing one or more of these things, they assure them that they are saved and going to heaven when they die and that there is no way they can lose their salvation.

This "other gospel" requires no obedience or submission to the authority of the King of the kingdom, Jesus the Christ, our Lord. In fact, this "other gospel" claims to have no cost at all; it is totally free, easy and painless. During the response to the presentation of this "other gospel," the people are often assured that they will not even be embarrassed by having to do anything in public. Often during this process, everyone is asked to bow their heads and close their eyes. Only the pastor's or the evangelist's eyes are open so they can make a head count and add the recorded number of notches to their salvation belt.

In order to deceive and inoculate the hearers against receiving the genuine gospel of the kingdom, this "other gospel" contains many elements of truth. However, a gospel without cost, a gospel without obedience and submission to the authority of the king, is a gospel with no scriptural basis at all. Nowhere in Scripture is an unbeliever told that, if they feel sorry for their sins and ask Jesus to come into their heart and be their savior, they will be saved and go to heaven.

"Repentance," or "repent," as used in Scripture in presenting the gospel of the kingdom to unbelievers does not mean to feel sorry for something, but rather it means to change your mind. To repent means to change your mind about the direction you are going in life, and to turn back to God by trusting in Jesus. To do this requires that you change your mind regarding what you think about Jesus.

Those that preach this "other gospel" present it as a gospel without cost, but, in reality, the cost of receiving this "other gospel" is devastatingly high. Those that respond to this "other gospel" are assured by those that preach it that they have eternal salvation. These "new believers" are thereby inoculated against the genuine gospel of the kingdom.

The god of this world has used this "other gospel" to blind their minds "that they might not see the light of the gospel of the glory of Christ, who is the image of God" (2 Corinthians 4:3-4). Every time the people who received

44

this "other gospel" hear the genuine gospel according to Scripture, the enemy of the gospel will assure them again that they are already saved. They will point them back to that time when they responded to this "other gospel." By doing this, the enemy of the gospel is able to keep them from ever responding to the genuine gospel of the kingdom, and thereby truly be saved.

There are many "other gospels," the gospel of salvation through water baptism, the gospel of salvation through good works, and so on. Each of these "other gospels" has the common feature that they deny the need to simply believe in their heart that God raised Jesus from the dead, establishing His authority as Lord and King (Matthew 28:18), and a complete voluntary submission to His authority, confessing Him as Lord.

Anyone who preaches "another gospel" or that assures another of their salvation is an enemy of the gospel. If a requirement of salvation is that we believe in our heart, how can we assure anyone of what is in their heart? Scripture says in Jeremiah 17:9, "The heart is more deceitful than all else and is desperately wicked; who can understand it? I, the Lord, search the heart, I test the mind, even to give each man according to his way, according to the results of his deeds."

Only God knows a person's heart, and only God can give anyone an assurance of salvation. He does this by the witness of His Holy Spirit that He causes to dwell within the believer. Romans 8:16 says, "The Spirit Himself testifies with our spirit that we are children of God." This Spirit dwelling in the believer teaches him about Christ and spreads the love of God abroad in the believer's heart. It is also by this love, the love that God gives the believer for the Christian brothers, that the person can be assured that they are saved. I John 3:14 says, "We know that we have passed out of death into life, because we love the brethren. He who does not love abides in death."

45

God wants believers to have an assurance that they are born again, that they are truly His children. However, God insists on being the only one His children look to for that assurance.

As we have seen previously, Scripture sets forth only one gospel that we are to preach, the same gospel the apostles preached, the gospel of the kingdom. This gospel presents Jesus as having been given all authority by virtue of His having been raised from the dead by the power of God, and the necessity of our submitting wholeheartedly to that authority in all obedience.

Romans 6:16-18 says, "Do you not know that when you present yourselves to someone as slaves for obedience, you are slaves of the one you obey, either of sin resulting in death, or of obedience resulting in righteousness? But thanks be to God that though you were slaves to sin, you became obedient from the heart to that form of teaching to which you were committed, and having been freed from sin, you became slaves of righteousness."

Anyone that preaches "another gospel" or assures another that they are saved is an enemy of the gospel. Are you an enemy of the gospel? If you are, or have been, I urge you to repent and return to the gospel of the kingdom, the gospel found in the Bible. Return to proclaiming salvation through faith in Jesus and His resurrection from the dead and submission to His authority, confessing Him as Lord. In doing this, you will become a fellow laborer with the apostles, building up the kingdom of God.

I strongly encourage you to read through all of the Scripture references given here. Search the Scriptures and see for yourself what gospel the apostles in the first century were proclaiming. Prayerfully seek understanding from God according to His Word. As you prayerfully search the Scriptures, if you are a believer, the indwelling Holy Spirit will teach you. He will enlighten your heart that you might understand and walk in His way.

My prayer is that this will stir up within you a desire to proclaim to all that Jesus has been raised from the dead, never to die again, and that all authority has been given unto Him (Matthew 28:18-20). May this gospel of the kingdom go forth into all the earth; then will come the end of the age (Matthew 24:14).

Chapter 5 Discussion Questions: Assurance of Salvation

1. What is the gospel of the kingdom?
2. How are we ushered into this kingdom?
3. How is the power of Satan broken?
4. What is "another gospel"?
5. What is the cost of receiving this "other gospel"?
6. Who is the enemy of the gospel?
7. Why should we not assure anyone that they are saved?
8. Who is the only one that can assure anyone that they are saved?
9. How does God assure someone that they are saved?
10. What should we do if we are or have been an enemy of the gospel?

Everything You Need

P aul warns the believers in 2 Corinthians 5:10, "For every one of us will have to stand without pretense before Christ our judge, and we shall be rewarded for what we did when we lived in our bodies, whether it was good or bad" (Phillips). At the coming judgment, we will have to give an account for how we lived.

The Apostle Paul proclaims in Philippians 2:9-11, "God highly exalted Him, and bestowed on Him the name which is above every name, that at the name of Jesus every knee should bow, of those who are in heaven and on earth and under the earth, and that every tongue should confess that Jesus Christ is Lord, to the glory of God the Father." At the coming judgment, many will try to give excuses for why we did not submit to the Lordship of Jesus Christ and live in obedience to Him.

Whatever our excuse, His response will be the same. "You are without excuse." Jesus will say to each of us, "I gave you everything you needed. You simply chose not to avail yourself of it. Rather, you chose to live according to your own understanding, in the foolishness of your own wisdom, rather than to humble yourself and to submit completely to me."

What excuse will you use? Perhaps you claim to be an atheist that does not believe there is a God. Romans 1:18-20 says, "For God's wrath is revealed from heaven against all godlessness and unrighteousness of people who by their unrighteousness suppress the truth, since what can be known about God is evident among them, because God has shown it to them. For His invisible attributes, that is, His eternal power and divine nature, have been clearly seen since the creation of the world, being understood through what He has made. As a result, people are without excuse." Jesus will say to the atheists, "You are without excuse. Through the testimony of all creation, I gave you everything you needed to believe there is a God and to honor Him as God."

Perhaps you believe there is a God and have even sought to worship Him as God in your own way. However, when you heard the good news about how God raised Jesus from the dead and made Him Lord of all, you didn't respond to the invitation to humble yourself and come to Jesus. Perhaps you didn't believe He was the only way to God. Perhaps you thought to yourself, "There must be another way. Surely all the other religions can't be wrong. What about the billions of Hindus, Buddhists, Muslims?"

You felt so philosophical and wise according to your own understanding. Yet Jesus said in John 14:6, "I am the way, the truth, and the life. No one comes to the Father except through me." Jesus was making it perfectly clear that He was the only way to the Father, and that all other ways were a lie and a deception. You, however, refused to believe Him. Jesus will say to these religious people, "You are without excuse. Through the testimony of Scripture and the witness of Christians, I gave you everything you needed to believe that I am the only way to the Father."

Maybe you just had so many things you wanted to do before making a commitment to Jesus. In Luke 14:16-21 Jesus told a parable to the religious leaders of His day saying: "A man was giving a large banquet and invited many. At the time of the banquet, he sent his slave to tell those who were invited, 'Come, because everything is now ready.' But without exception they all began to make excuses. The first one said to him, 'I have bought a field, and I must go out and see it. I ask you to excuse me.' Another said, 'I have bought five yoke of oxen, and I'm going to try them out. I ask you to excuse me.' And another said, 'I just got married, and therefore I'm unable to come.' So the slave came back and reported these things to his master. Then in anger, the master of the house told his slave, 'Go out quickly into the streets and alleys of the city, and bring in here the poor, maimed, blind, and lame!'" (HCSB). Perhaps you were too busy to listen and obey.

Romans 10:17-18 says, "So faith comes from what is heard, and what is heard comes through the message about Christ. But I ask, 'Did they not hear?' Yes, they did: Their voice has gone out to all the earth, and their words to the ends of the inhabited world" (HCSB). So Jesus will say to those that did not respond to the good news and the invitation to come to Him saying, "You are without excuse. I gave you everything you needed by causing the good news about My being raised from the dead and being made Lord of all to go out throughout the entire world. This word was spread to the ends of the inhabited world."

Perhaps you are one that has responded to the invitation to come to Jesus. Believing that God raised Jesus from the dead and made Him both Lord and Christ, you were born again and were filled with the Holy Spirit. However, you did not walk in obedience to Him, in righteousness and true holiness. Perhaps you tried as hard as you could, attempting by the flesh to complete what was begun in the Spirit, but you found it to be just too difficult. So you simply gave up and went back to your old ways.

In Matthew 25:14-30 Jesus speaks to His disciples telling them a parable about the kingdom of heaven saying: "For it is just like a man about to go on a journey, who called his own slaves and entrusted his possessions to them. To one he gave five talents, to another, two, and to another, one, each according to his own ability; and he went on his journey. Immediately the one who had received the five talents went and traded with them, and gained five more talents. In the same manner the one who had received the two talents gained two more. But he who received the one talent went away, and dug a hole in the ground and hid his master's money.

"Now after a long time the master of those slaves came and settled accounts with them. The one who had received the five talents came up and brought five more talents, saying, 'Master, you entrusted five talents to me. See, I have gained five more talents.' His master said to him, 'Well done, good and faithful slave. You were faithful with a few things, I will put you in charge of many things; enter into the joy of your master.'

"Also the one who had received the two talents came up and said, 'Master, you entrusted two talents to me. See, I have gained two more talents.' His master said to him, 'Well done, good and faithful slave. You were faithful with a few things, I will put you in charge of many things; enter into the joy of your master.'

"And the one also who had received the one talent came up and said, 'Master, I knew you to be a hard man, reaping where you did not sow and gathering where you scattered no seed. And I was afraid, and went away and hid your talent in the ground. See, you have what is yours.'

"But his master answered and said to him, 'You wicked, lazy slave, you knew that I reap where I did not sow and gather where I scattered no seed. Then you ought to have put my money in the bank, and on my arrival I would have received my money back with interest. Therefore take away the talent from him, and give it to the one who has the ten talents.'

"'For to everyone who has, more shall be given, and he will have an abundance; but from the one who does not have, even what he does have shall be taken away. Throw out the worthless slave into the outer darkness; in that place there will be weeping and gnashing of teeth.'" The master was angry because the slave did not believe that he had been given everything needed to serve his master faithfully.

2 Peter 1:3-11 assures us saying: "His divine power has granted to us everything pertaining to life and godliness,

through the true knowledge of Him who called us by His own glory and excellence. For by these He has granted to us His precious and magnificent promises, so that by them you may become partakers of the divine nature, having escaped the corruption that is in the world by lust. Now for this very reason also, applying all diligence, in your faith supply moral excellence, and in your moral excellence, knowledge, and in your knowledge, self-control, and in your self-control, perseverance, and in your perseverance, godliness, and in your godliness, brotherly kindness, and in your brotherly kindness, love. For if these qualities are yours and are increasing, they render you neither useless nor unfruitful in the true knowledge of our Lord Jesus Christ. For he who lacks these qualities is blind or short-sighted, having forgotten his purification from his former sins.

"Therefore, brethren, be all the more diligent to make certain about His calling and choosing you; for as long as you practice these things, you will never stumble; for in this way the entrance into the eternal kingdom of our Lord and Savior Jesus Christ will be abundantly supplied to you" (NIV). To those believers that do not live godly lives, Jesus will say, "You are without excuse. I gave you everything you needed to live godly lives. Why didn't you use it?"

1 Peter 1:13-25 commands us saying, "Therefore, with minds that are alert and fully sober, set your hope on the grace to be brought to you when Jesus Christ is revealed at his coming. As obedient children, do not conform to the evil desires you had when you lived in ignorance. But just as he who called you is holy, so be holy in all you do; for it is written: 'Be holy, because I am holy.'

"Since you call on a Father who judges each person's work impartially, live out your time as foreigners here in reverent fear. For you know that it was not with perishable things such as silver or gold that you were redeemed from the empty way of life handed down to you from your ancestors, but with the precious blood of Christ, a lamb without blemish or defect. He was chosen before the creation of the world, but was revealed in these last times for your sake. Through him you believe in God, who raised him from the dead and glorified him, and so your faith and hope are in God.

"Now that you have purified yourselves by obeying the truth so that you have sincere love for each other, love one another deeply, from the heart. For you have been born again, not of perishable seed, but of imperishable, through the living and enduring word of God. For, 'All people are like grass, and all their glory is like the flowers of the field; the grass withers and the flowers fall, but the word of the Lord endures forever.' And this is the word that was preached to you" (NIV). The Lord has given us everything we need pertaining to life and godliness.

What is the one thing God requires of every born-again believer? God requires that we love one another. Jesus said in John 15:12: "This is My commandment, that you love one another, just as I have loved you." This is God's one basic requirement for every believer. There are no exceptions.

If you are not fulfilling this basic requirement, it does not matter what else you might do for God, it is all meaningless and of no value. You may be a great evangelist, the pastor of a large church, a missionary to some distant land, a Sunday school teacher. You may have the gift of prophecy, or you may heal the sick, but as 1 Corinthians 13:3 says, "If I give all my possessions to feed the poor, and if I surrender my body to be burned, but do not have love, it profits me nothing."

I John 3:16-18 instructs us saying, "This is how we know what love is: Jesus Christ laid down his life for us. And we ought to lay down our lives for our brothers and sisters. If anyone has material possessions and sees a brother or sister in need but has no pity on them, how can the love of God be in that person? Dear children, let us not love with words or speech but with actions and in truth."

It is only when we have fulfilled God's command to love one another, that we will have boldness to stand before Him, and will not have to make any excuses. 1 John 4:17-21 says, "By this, love is perfected with us, so that we may have confidence in the day of judgment; because as He is, so also are we in this world. There is no fear in love; but perfect love casts out fear, because fear involves punishment, and the one who fears is not perfected in love. We love, because He first loved us.

"If someone says, 'I love God,' and hates his brother, he is a liar; for the one who does not love his brother whom he has seen, cannot love God whom he has not seen. And this commandment we have from Him, that the one who loves God should love his brother also."

The real test of loving one another, for any believer, is whether they love the person that God has placed nearest to them. For many of us, this person would be our spouse. It is for this reason God has given very specific instructions in the Scriptures as to how a husband is to treat his wife, and how a wife is to treat her husband.

It is easy to love someone that you have no dealings with. It is difficult, however, to love someone that is always near us. They are the ones that are most likely to do things that offend us and cause us discomfort, and sometimes even bitterness. So the real test is, how do I treat this person that God has placed right here next to me? How do I treat my spouse? I say I love God, but do I love this brother or sister that God has placed right here next to me? If not, then I cannot love God.

Ephesians 5:25 says, "Husbands, love your wives, just as Christ also loved the church and gave Himself up for her." Colossians 3:19 instructs us saying, "Husbands, love your wives and do not be embittered against them." 1 Peter 3:7 says, "You husbands in the same way, live with *your wives* in an understanding way, as with someone weaker, since she is a woman; and show her honor as a fellow heir of the grace of life, so that your prayers will not be hindered."

Ephesians 5:22 says, "Wives, be subject to your own husbands, as to the Lord." Paul writes in Titus 2:3-5 saying: "Older women likewise are to...encourage the young women to love their husbands, to love their children, to be sensible, pure, workers at home, kind, being subject to their own husbands, so that the word of God will not be dishonored." 1 Peter 3:1 instructs wives saying, "In the same way, you wives, be submissive to your own husbands so that even if any *of them* are disobedient to the word, they may be won without a word by the behavior of their wives."

God's love and God's life will lead each husband and wife to seek to please their spouse. This will be the evidence that we are in fact being led by the Spirit. Our focus will be more on pleasing our spouse than ourselves. Paul refers to this as the expected situation in a marriage. In 1 Corinthians 7:33-34 he says that the husband will be concerned about "how he may please his wife," and the wife will be concerned about "how she may please her husband."

The Scriptures command husbands to demonstrate their love for their wives by providing them with everything they need, including understanding, gentleness and affection, just as Christ does unto the church. The Scriptures also command women to demonstrate their love for their husbands by submitting to them as unto the Lord, with kindness and honor, just as Christ did unto the Father.

How can we live in such continually loving relationships with our spouses? In our own strength it is not possible. However, God quickens us. God strengthens us. God equips us. He gives us everything we need to live godly lives, but He expects "us" to do it. It is true that apart from Christ we can do nothing. However, if we have been joined to Christ and are one spirit with Him, then there is nothing that God requires us to do that we are not able to do.

Paul says in Philippians 4:13, "I can do all things through Him who strengthens me." If I have heard Christ, as the indwelling Spirit, speaking to me, instructing me to do something, there is no reason for me to sit idly by and wait for God to do something in my life. I can do all things that He requires of me through Jesus Christ who strengthens me. I do not need to wait. I have no excuse. Through Christ as the indwelling Spirit, I have everything I need. I simply need to trust Christ to empower me to do whatever God requires of me.

This is true spirituality, having an ear to hear, and a heart to obey. True spirituality is a godly life lived boldly, without fear and without excuses, in full obedience and full submission to the Lord, Jesus Christ. This life is lived by faith, believing that Christ is able to empower the believer to do everything that God requires.

Praise God! What a Christ we have! Let us look to Him in faith, believing He is able. He will empower, equip, and strengthen us to do everything God requires of us. Then we will be able to say with Paul, "I have fought the good fight, I have finished the course, I have kept the faith; in the future there is laid up for me the crown of righteousness, which the Lord, the righteous Judge, will award to me on that day; and not only to me, but also to all who have loved His appearing" (2 Timothy 4:6-8).

Chapter 6 Discussion Questions: Everything You Need

1. What Christians will have to stand before the judgment seat of Christ?
2. At the judgment seat, why might Jesus say that we are without excuse?
3. What response might Jesus have to excuses made by atheists?
4. What response might Jesus have to excuses made by religious people?
5. What response might Jesus have to excuses made by unfruitful Christians?

6. What response might Jesus have to excuses made by Christians that failed to live godly lives?

7. What is the one thing God requires of every born-again believer?

8. What is the real test of loving one another?

9. How can we live in such continually loving relationships with our spouses?

10. What is true spirituality?

11. What do we need to live lives wholly pleasing to God that is not available in Christ?

A God of Order

"No creature is hidden from Him, but all things are naked and exposed to the eyes of Him to whom we must give an account" (Hebrews 4:13, HCSB).

A s we have already seen, the Scriptures make it very clear that we will all be held accountable for the things we do. We will all have to give an account of ourselves to God (Romans 14:12). It is important that each of us understands this fact. If we do understand it, that understanding will have a tremendous impact on how we live our lives, both in relation to the world around us, and in relation to God and His church.

It is also essential that we understand that the God who will judge each of us is a God of order. God has established a very clear system of authority for all of creation. This order, especially as it pertains to the Christian believer, is clearly set forth in 1 Corinthians 11:3. Here Paul writes: "But I want you to know that Christ is the head of every man, and the man is the head of the woman, and God is the head of Christ" (HCSB).

As we have previously discussed, a clear indication of whether a man is truly submitted to Christ is whether he is loving his wife as Christ loved the church. Ephesians 5:25-29 says, "Husbands, love your wives, just as Christ also loved the church and gave Himself up for her, so that he might sanctify her, having cleansed her by the washing of water with the word, that He might present to Himself the church in all her glory, having no spot or wrinkle or any such thing; but that she would be holy and blameless. So husbands should also love their wives as their own bodies. He who loves his own wife loves himself; for no one ever hated his own flesh, but nourishes and cherishes it, just as Christ also does the church."

Also, a clear indication of whether a woman is truly submitted to Christ is whether she is submitted to her own husband as to the Lord. Ephesians 5:22-24 says, "Wives, be subject to your own husbands, as to the Lord. For the husband is the head of the wife, as Christ also is the head of the church, He Himself being the Savior of the body. But as the church is subject to Christ, so also the wives ought to be to their husbands in everything."

God has also given us specific instructions concerning the believer's relationship to authority at every level. Romans 13:1-2 says "Every person is to be in subjection to the governing authorities. For there is no authority except from God, and those which exist are established by God. Therefore, whoever resists authority has opposed the ordinances of God, and those who have opposed will receive condemnation upon themselves."

1 Peter 2:17 instructs us, "Honor everyone. Love the brotherhood. Fear God. Honor the emperor" (HCSB). When Peter wrote this passage, Nero was emperor. Nero was possibly the most ruthless ruler in the history of mankind, especially in his persecution of Christians. Yet, Peter commands the Christians to honor the emperor.

Peter continues in the next verse to instruct the believers saying, "Household slaves, submit yourselves to your masters with all respect, not only to the good and gentle but also to the cruel" (HCSB). Peter explains in the next verse, "For it brings favor if, because of conscience toward God, someone endures grief from suffering unjustly" (HCSB).

Paul goes even further in Acts 23:5. Here Paul has just been illegally struck in the face by order of the high priest. Paul responds in anger, threatening the high priest, telling him that God would strike him. Those standing by warned Paul against speaking against the high priest. Paul responds saying, "I did not know brothers that it was the high priest. For it is

written, 'You must not speak evil of a ruler of your people'"
(HCSB). Paul was quoting from Exodus 22:28.

Not only are believers commanded to submit to all rulers
that are in positions of authority over them, they are to submit
with all respect. We are not even to speak evil of any ruler, no
matter how much we may dislike their policies, practices, or
their person.

Children are to submit to their parents. Employees are
to submit to their employers. Everyone is to submit to the
governing authorities. Wives are to submit to their own husbands. Men are to submit to Christ. God is a God of order. He
has established a specific structure of authority for everyone.
There is not a person in this world that is not required to
submit respectfully to the authority that God has established
over him. There are no exceptions.

In addition to this specific structure of authority, God has
established certain principles to guide our living. One of these
principles is set forth in 1 Corinthians 14:32-33, where Paul
again writes saying: "And the prophets' spirits are under the
control of the prophets, since God is not a God of disorder
but of peace."

This principle is also seen in Ephesians 5:15-21 where
Paul warns us saying: "Pay careful attention, then, to how you
walk—not as unwise people but as wise—making the most
of the time, because the days are evil. So don't be foolish,
but understand what the Lord's will is. And don't get drunk
with wine, which leads to reckless actions, but be filled by the
Spirit: speaking to one another in psalms, hymns, and spiritual
songs, singing and making music from your heart to the Lord,
giving thanks always for everything to God the Father in the
name of our Lord Jesus Christ, submitting to one another in
the fear of Christ" (HCSB).

Here we see the result of doing something to excess,
of doing something to the point that it takes control of you.
Getting drunk on wine is the result of drinking wine to excess.
The problem with drinking wine to excess is that it results in

reckless actions. In other words, it results in us losing control of our bodies, and the actions that we take with our bodies. When we are drunk, we are no longer in control. This violates a basic principle of God. He requires that we always maintain control of our bodies, and of the actions that we take with our bodies.

We are never to let our body's desire for anything be catered to, to the extent that we lose control over our own body. Allowing an excess of anything our body desires will eventually cause us to lose control. This will result in reckless actions. This principle not only applies to the various lusts and desires by which our body tries to take over and have control of us, it also applies to things in the spiritual realm.

We are not puppets. We are not robots. We are not to yield control of ourselves to anything. We are always to be in control of ourselves. Neither the Spirit nor our body is to be in control over us. It is critically important that we understand this principle. We are never to allow anything to take control over us.

. In 1 Corinthians 6:12 Paul tells us: "'Everything is permissible for me,' but not everything is helpful. 'Everything is permissible for me,' but I will not be brought under the control of anything" (HCSB). In 1 Corinthians 9:27 he says: "I discipline my body and bring it under strict control, so that after preaching to others, I myself will not be disqualified" (HCSB). Galatians 5:22-23 reads: "But the fruit of the Spirit is love, joy, peace, patience, kindness, goodness, faithfulness, gentleness, self-control; against such things there is no law."

Notice here that the fruit of the Spirit is, among other things, self-control. In other words, when a believer is being led by the Spirit, the Spirit will produce self-control in that believer's life. Self-control is a fruit produced by the Spirit in a believer's life as the believer yields to the leading of the Spirit. The Spirit does not control the believer. The believer, rather, continually chooses to follow the leading of the Spirit.

There are some, who claim to be Christians, who believe that one sign of spirituality is to allow one's self to be fully under the control of the Spirit. This submission to the full control of the Spirit is then demonstrated in various ways. Among these is the practice of being "slain in the Spirit" whereby the so-called believer simply collapses to the floor as a result of the Spirit's "touch." Other manifestations of being under the control of the Spirit are uncontrolled shouting, singing, barking, jumping, dancing, and any other "uncontrolled" behavior.

Let me be very clear about this. Any uncontrolled behavior, that is any action that we commit because we are unable to control ourselves, is not of God. 1 Corinthians 14:33 reminds us: "God is not a God of disorder" (HCSB). When we are being led by the Spirit, that Spirit will produce self-control in our lives. According to Scripture, self-control in the life of a Christian is a basic and necessary sign of spiritual growth. A lack of self-control is clear evidence that we are not walking by the Spirit.

Paul sets forth the requirements of a Christian brother that desires to serve the Lord in a position of responsibility for the well-being of the church. In 1 Timothy 3:1-3 he writes: "If anyone aspires to be an overseer, he desires a noble work. An overseer, therefore, must be above reproach, the husband of one wife, self-controlled, sensible, respectable, hospitable, an able teacher, not addicted to wine, not a bully but gentle, not quarrelsome, not greedy" (HCSB). A basic requirement for this Christian man is self-control.

We see this same requirement for Christian women. Paul writes in Titus 2:3-5 instructing them: "In the same way, older women are to be reverent in behavior, not slanderers, not addicted to much wine. They are to teach what is good, so they may encourage the young women to love their husbands and to love their children, to be self-controlled, pure, homemakers, kind, and submissive to their husbands, so that God's message will not be slandered" (HCSB).

Self-control means that we are in control of our own bodies. We are responsible for the actions we take. Our bodies must not control us. We, the human being, the soul within the body, must be in control. This is a basic principle of the Christian life. We must not allow anything to take control over us. Not our body, not the Spirit, nothing can be allowed to control our actions. We must be self-controlled at all times.

Our bodies have many natural desires, urges, or hungers. We have natural hungers for food, drink, sex, and so on. These desires can be very strong. There are times that they seem to be almost uncontrollable. There are some people that have realized that they are weak and are susceptible to being controlled by these desires or lusts. Some of these people have developed a policy of legalism, fearing, that if they give in even the slightest amount to one of these desires, they will not be able to control it.

Colossians 2:20-23 talks about such practices and their futility in controlling these fleshly desires of our bodies. It says: "If you have died with Christ to the elementary principles of the world, why, as if you were living in the world, do you submit yourself to decrees, such as, 'Do not handle, do not taste, do not touch!' (which all *refer to* things destined to perish with use)—in accordance with the commandments and teachings of men? These are matters which have, to be sure, the appearance of wisdom in self-made religion and self-abasement and severe treatment of the body, *but are* of no value against fleshly indulgence."

This policy of denying the body any satisfaction of its natural desires is not scriptural. On the contrary, Scripture tells us clearly that this practice is of no benefit against these desires. These natural desires of the body need to be tended to, but they need to be tended to in a controlled and moderate way. These natural desires of the body are desires that God has placed within us, and by the leading of His Spirit He will direct us on how to satisfy these desires in a godly and controlled manner.

These hungers were placed within us by God, and, as such, they are not in themselves evil. God has provided safe, healthy, controllable ways for us to satisfy these basic natural hungers. Satisfying these hungers in a moderate, godly fashion will result in a happy, healthy life. Not satisfying these hungers in the ways that God has provided will result in lives of hardship, frustration, and excess. Left unsatisfied, these natural desires will become lusts that will try to take control of us.

Uncontrolled eating is gluttony. Uncontrolled drinking is drunkenness. Proverbs 23:19-21 says: "Listen, my son, and be wise; keep your mind on the right course. Don't associate with those who drink too much wine or with those who gorge themselves on meat. For the drunkard and the glutton will become poor, and grogginess will clothe them in rags" (HCSB).

Uncontrolled sexual activity is sexual immorality. It will result in heartbreak, sickness and confusion. 1 Corinthians 6:18 warns us: "The person who is sexually immoral sins against his own body." God has provided us with very controlled, moderate, and yet, totally satisfying ways to address all of these natural desires.

We are able to address these natural desires of the body in a controlled and satisfying way if we are walking by the Spirit. Galatians 5:16 promises: "Walk by the Spirit, and you won't fulfill the lust of the flesh" (WEB). When we deny the natural desires of our body, these desires grow to become lusts, and they become so strong that we become controlled by them. It is critically important that we live our lives being led by the Spirit, then these lusts will not control us. Rather, we will be in control of our bodies.

God does not want us to be gluttons, drunkards, or sexually immoral. The Corinthians wrote to Paul about the issue of sexual activity. Paul responds to their questions in 1 Corinthians 7:1-5 writing: "Now concerning the things about which you wrote, it is good for a man not to touch a woman. But because of immoralities, each man is to have his own wife, and each woman is to have her own husband.

"The husband must fulfill his duty to his wife, and likewise also the wife to her husband. The wife does not have authority over her own body, but the husband *does*; and likewise also the husband does not have authority over his own body, but the wife *does*. Stop depriving one another, except by agreement for a time, so that you may devote yourselves to prayer, and come together again so that Satan will not tempt you because of your lack of self-control."

It is clear from this passage that a strong sexual appetite is natural, and that God has provided a safe, healthy, and moderate way for us to satisfy that appetite. That way is for each man to have his own wife, and for each woman to have her own husband. When either spouse is withholding themselves from the other, this deprivation can cause a lack of self-control and lust that looks for satisfaction outside of the marriage. Again, as with food and drink, a good appetite is healthy and is satisfied by God's provision and God's arrangement, but excess is unhealthy and depravation leads to lust.

It is amazing how much enjoyment we can experience in the Christian life when we understand that God is a God of order. "Christ is the head of every man, and the man is the head of the woman, and God is the head of Christ." When we are led by the Spirit, the Spirit will produce fruit in our lives. A significant part of the fruit that the Spirit produces in the life of a believer is self-control. If we are walking by the Spirit, our lives should be a testimony of self-control. This self-control will result in the godly enjoyment of the many blessings that God has bestowed upon us, and not a life of legalistic asceticism, or in a life of uncontrolled behavior.

Jesus says in John 10:10, "I came that they might have life, and have it abundantly." He gives His joy unto us that our joy may be full. In John 15:11 Jesus tells us, "These things I have spoken unto you so that My joy may be in you, and that your joy may be made full." God is good. He wants the very best for us. When we walk with Him, being led by the Spirit, we will not fulfill the lust of the flesh, but we will be empowered by the Spirit to live godly lives of self-control, fully satisfied with God's rich provision for our every need.

Chapter 7 Discussion Questions:
A God of Order

1. Who is hidden from Him to whom we must give account?
2. What does Paul say in I Corinthians 11:3 is God's system of order?
3. What is a clear indication of whether a man is truly submitted to Christ?
4. What is a clear indication of whether a woman is truly submitted to Christ?
5. What instructions has God given concerning the believer's relationship to authority at every level?
6. Who is not required to submit respectfully to the authority that God has established over him?
7. What is a basic principal of God concerning the actions that we take with our bodies?
8. What is a lack of self-control evidence of?
9. What is the benefit of the legalistic practices of asceticism, touch not, taste not, handle not?
10. What will be the result of not satisfying the natural hungers of the body in the ways that God has provided?
11. What has God provided for us to satisfy our sexual appetite in a safe, healthy and moderate way?
12. What does the depravation of the natural appetites that God placed in us lead to?

The Mind-set of the Spirit

⟋⟍

Romans 8:9 states: "if anyone does not have the Spirit of Christ, he does not belong to Him." This verse also makes it clear that if you have been born again, if you have the Spirit of Christ living in you: "you, however, are not in the flesh, but in the Spirit, since the Spirit of God lives in you."

According to this verse, whether we are in the Spirit or not, is not dependent on our mind-set or conduct, whether spiritual or fleshly, but rather is dependent on whether God has placed us in Christ. We are in the Spirit because the Spirit of Christ is dwelling within us. We are there because God placed us in Christ when He placed the Spirit of Christ in us. 1 Corinthians 1:30 proclaims, "By His doing you are in Christ Jesus."

If we are born again, if the Spirit of God is dwelling in us, we are in the Spirit. It is, however, very important how we think, what mind-set we have. Romans 8:6 says, "For the mind-set of the flesh is death, but the mind-set of the Spirit is life and peace" (HCSB). Even though we are in the Spirit, in order to be obedient to the leading of the Spirit, we must have the mind-set of the Spirit, understanding the reality of spiritual things. We must see things from the perspective of our being in the Spirit and of the blessings and empowerment that are ours in the Spirit. This mind-set of the Spirit results in life and peace, and enables us to walk by faith.

However, if our mind-set is of the flesh, understanding things according to the flesh and according to our abilities and strengths in the flesh, we will experience death. The mind-set of the flesh sees things according to the ability and nature of the flesh. It is hostile to God because it does not submit itself to God's law, for it is unable to do so.

In the mind-set of the flesh, we have fear and weakness. We fear that anything "we" do will be of the flesh, of our self, of our own righteousness. This mind-set of the flesh causes us to be like the person with the one talent, who, because of his fears, fails to invest his talent. He therefore bears no fruit for his Master, and, as a result, suffers tremendous loss. Remember the parable of the talents (Matthew 25:14-30).

This fear that we experience when we have the mind-set of the flesh can actually paralyze us, keeping us from doing even the most basic functions of a normal responsible life. It may even cause us to be afraid to pursue our given occupation, fearing that doing so would be a demonstration of self-reliance and a lack of faith in God and His provision for us.

When we have the mind-set of the flesh, we are unable to please God, because we see things according to the ability of the flesh and not according to the ability of God in the Spirit. Without faith, it is impossible to please God. When we have the mind-set of the flesh, we do not think in terms of faith and the Spirit, but rather in terms of the flesh.

Also, there are many times when the mind-set of the flesh causes us to see the spiritual life of the believer in a very convoluted way. It may cause us to think that we are spiritual only when we are doing or saying "spiritual" things. Perhaps it will cause us to think, that in order to be spiritual, we must be reading the Scriptures, preaching the gospel, or working full-time as a pastor or an evangelist. You can do all of these things and still not have the mind-set of the Spirit.

On the other hand, we can be doing the most mundane activities of life, and have the mind-set of the Spirit. We can be cleaning the house, baking bread, disciplining our children, mowing the grass, or just working at our job, whatever it may be, and do so with the mind-set of the Spirit.

The Lord does not empower us by the indwelling Spirit just to do "spiritual" things. He empowers us by the indwelling of the Spirit to enable us to live the ordinary life in this flesh in a holy manner. He enables us to be over-comers as we endure all of the struggles and trials of everyday life.

He empowers us by the indwelling Spirit to love the brothers, to provide for our family, to work to produce excess so we can provide for the needs of others, to provide hospitality, to visit the sick, to give food to the hungry and to give clothing to the naked. God is glorified when we live our routine daily lives in the glory of His presence. To do this, we need to know Him, and the tremendous blessings He has freely given us by His Spirit indwelling our spirit.

In Matthew 13:18-23 the parable of the sower shows us the importance of not just hearing the word, but of understanding it. It says, "Hear then the parable of the sower. When anyone hears the word of the kingdom and does not understand it, the evil one comes and snatches away what has been sown in his heart. This is the one on whom seed was sown beside the road. The one on whom seed was sown on the rocky places, this is the man who hears the word and immediately receives it with joy; yet he has no firm root in himself, but is only temporary, and when affliction or persecution arises because of the word, immediately he falls away.

"And the one on whom the seed was sown among the thorns, this is the man who hears the word, and the worry of the world, and the deceitfulness of wealth choke the word, and it becomes unfruitful. And the one on whom seed was sown on the good soil, this is the man who hears the word and understands it; who indeed bears fruit and brings forth, some a hundredfold, some sixty, and some thirty."

The enemy is able to come and snatch away what is sown in the heart of the one who lacks understanding. However, the one that hears the word, and understands the word, bears much fruit. The enemy does all he can to keep us from understanding the word. He does not want us to know the blessings that are ours in the realm of the Spirit wherein God has placed us in Christ. He does not want us to know that God is good, and that God wants the very best for us.

This is why it is imperative that the believer has the eyes of his understanding opened, that he would have the mind-set of the Spirit, and not the mind-set of the flesh. That is why Paul prays for us in Ephesians 1:16-19 that God would give us "a spirit of wisdom and revelation in the knowledge of Him" (HCSB).

He prays that the eyes of our "heart might be enlightened so we might know the hope of His calling, the glorious riches of His inheritance in the saints, and the immeasurable greatness of His power to us who believe, according to the working of His vast strength" (HCSB). This understanding gives us the mind-set of the Spirit, which is essential to pleasing God and to walking worthy of His calling.

In Ephesians 4:17-6:20 Paul sets forth commandments revealing God's expectations of how a believer is to live. Some of these are, "Walk no longer just as the Gentiles walk, in the futility of their mind...lay aside the old self...be renewed in the spirit of your mind and put on the new self... laying aside falsehood, speak truth...do not grieve the Holy Spirit...be kind to one another...walk in love...be careful how you walk...making the most of your time...be filled with the Spirit...put on the full armor of God...stand firm...pray at all times in the Spirit." We are expected to walk according to these commandments, empowered by the mind-set of the Spirit, realizing that everything that God requires from us is within our ability, as we look to Jesus and experience the greatness of His power working in and through us according to the working of His vast strength.

Galatians 2:20 concisely summarizes this life that we are to live. "I am crucified with Christ; and it is no longer I who live, but it is Christ who lives in me; and the life which I now live in the flesh I live in faith, the faith of the Son of God, who loved me and gave Himself up for me." This is exactly what Paul was referring to in Ephesians 4:20-24, and Colossians 3:9-11. There he talks about our having put off the old man, and putting on the new man, as we are being renewed in the spirit of our minds.

Again, in Colossians 1:9-14, Paul prays for us, that we might "be filled with the knowledge of His will in all wisdom and spiritual understanding, so that you may walk worthy of the Lord, pleasing to Him, bearing fruit in every good work and growing in the knowledge of God" (HCSB). He prays that we would "be strengthened with all power according to His glorious might." Again, this understanding gives us the mind-set of the Spirit, which is essential to pleasing God and to walking worthy of His calling.

In Colossians 3:5-4:6, Paul again gives us commandments revealing God's expectations of how a believer is to live. Some of these are, "Put them all aside: anger, wrath, malice, slander, and abusive speech from your mouth...put on a heart of compassion, kindness, humility, gentleness, and patience; bearing with one another and forgiving each other...let the peace of Christ rule in your hearts...let the word of Christ richly dwell in you...wives, be subject to your husbands...husbands, love your wives...conduct yourselves with wisdom toward outsiders...let your speech always be with grace." We are expected to walk according to these commandments, empowered by the mind-set of the Spirit, realizing that everything God requires from us is within our ability, as we look to Jesus and experience the greatness of His power working in and through us.

Seeking to walk according to these commandments is not placing us under the law, because our seeking to fulfill them is not according to the mind-set of the flesh. It is not looking to our own ability according to the understanding of the old man, but rather it is according to the mind-set of the Spirit. This is a mind-set that knows God and believes God. It relies on God to strengthen us according to the working of His mighty power by the Christ that dwells in us. This is the walk of faith that pleases God and produces in us life and peace.

Hebrews 4:1-3 speaks of the rest that God has prepared for His people, and how he expects His people to enter into His rest. It says, "Therefore, let us fear if, while a promise remains of entering His rest, any one of you may seem to have come short of it. For indeed we have had good news preached to us, just as they also; but the word they heard did not profit them, because it was not united by faith in those who heard. For we who have believed enter that rest."

The mind-set of the Spirit is what enables us to enter into the rest God has prepared for us. It is the mind-set of the flesh, the heart of unbelief, which prevents us from entering into God's rest. It is, therefore, essential that when a believer comes to know God, or rather, to be known by God, that he receives a thorough understanding of all the spiritual blessings that are his in Christ.

In order to receive this understanding, it is necessary that we are being renewed in the spirit of our minds. This enables us to put off the old man and the mind-set of the flesh, and to put on the new man with the mind-set of the Spirit. Ephesians 4:24 says this new man is created according to God's likeness in righteousness and holiness. This renewing of the spirit of our mind, with the resulting mind-set of the Spirit, enables us, through an understanding of the empowering of Christ by the indwelling Spirit, to live holy lives, walking worthy of the Lord, in obedience to Christ.

Paul says in 2 Corinthians 10:3-5: "Although we are walking in the flesh, we do not wage war in a fleshly way, since the weapons of our warfare are not fleshly, but are powerful through God for the demolition of strongholds. We demolish arguments and every high-minded thing that is raised up against the knowledge of God, taking every thought captive to the obedience of Christ" (HCSB).

Submission to Christ as Lord, and obedience to the leading of the Spirit are essential in the Christian life. To know His leading, we must know Him. According to 2 Peter 1:2-4, grace and peace is multiplied to us "through the knowledge of God and of Jesus Christ our Lord. For His divine power has given us everything required for life and godliness, through the knowledge of Him who called us by His own glory and goodness. By these He has given us very great and precious promises, so that through them we may share in the divine nature, escaping the corruption that is in the world because of evil desires" (HCSB).

The epistles in the New Testament are filled with instructions and commandments concerning how we are expected to live. Our spirit, through the indwelling of the Spirit of Christ, is filled with everything we need to live in full obedience, not as under the law, but as overflowing with the Spirit in all grace, love, joy, and peace. This is the fruit of the Spirit. This is the life lived out from the mind-set of the Spirit. This is to walk by the Spirit.

May our eyes be fixed on Jesus, the author and perfecter of our faith. May His joy be our joy, and may His blessings be fully experienced in our lives and in the life of every believer!

Chapter 8 Discussion Questions: The Mind-set of the Spirit

1. What is necessary for us to have to belong to Christ?
2. What is required for someone to be in the Spirit?
3. How do we get in Christ?
4. Why is it necessary to have the mind-set of the Spirit?
5. What effect does the mind-set of the flesh have on a believer?
6. What does the Lord empower us by the indwelling Spirit to do?
7. Why is it important to understand the word?
8. Why is it imperative that the believer has the eyes of his understanding opened?

9. Why is it necessary that the believer be filled with the knowledge of God's will?

10. What enables us to enter into the rest that God has prepared for us?

11. What does the renewing of our minds accomplish for us?

12. What actions are essential in the Christian life?

Love and Forgiveness

G od's love is unconditional. There is nothing that we need to do to earn it. John 3:16-17 says: "For God so loved the world, that He gave His only begotten Son, that whoever believes in Him shall not perish, but have eternal life. For God did not send the Son into the world to judge the world, but that the world might be saved through Him."

Romans 5:8 tells us: "God demonstrates His own love toward us, in that while we were yet sinners, Christ died for us." God did not wait for us to get our act together. He did not wait until we got ourselves all cleaned up. While we were still sinners, God sent His only Son to die for us.

Clearly, God's love is unconditional, but His forgiveness is not. There are certain requirements that must be met before God will forgive our sins. Jesus fulfilled most of these requirements, but we must fulfill the others.

The first requirement for the forgiveness of sins is that there must be a shedding of blood. Hebrews 9:22 says: "And according to the Law, *one may* almost *say*, all things are cleansed with blood, and without shedding of blood there is no forgiveness." This shedding of blood must be by a sacrifice that is without spot, unblemished.

This is why it was so important that Jesus lived a sinless life while on this earth. Only the blood of a sinless sacrifice would avail to satisfy the requirements of God's holy law. Hebrews 4:15 referring to Jesus says: "One who has been tempted in all things as *we are, yet* without sin."

Before being crucified, Jesus told His disciples that by His death His blood would be shed for the forgiveness of sins. In Matthew 26:27-28, when Jesus "had taken a cup and given thanks, He gave *it* to them, saying, 'Drink from it, all of you; for this is My blood of the covenant, which is poured out for many for forgiveness of sins.'"

Jesus, through His death on the cross, fully satisfied this requirement for the forgiveness of sins. Jesus, as a sinless sacrifice, fully satisfied God's requirement. Now the holy God had a basis upon which He could freely forgive sins. However, for any person's sins to be forgiven, there was still one requirement that must be satisfied.

Through His death on the cross, Jesus paid the full price for our redemption. However, for that redemption to be credited to our account, it is required that we enter, as a willing party, into that transaction. For us to be able to enter into this transaction and receive the forgiveness of sins for which Jesus died, we need to identify ourselves with Him.

Leviticus 4:27-31 says: "Now if anyone of the common people sins unintentionally in doing any of the things which the LORD has commanded not to be done, and becomes guilty, if his sin which he has committed is made known to him, then he shall bring for his offering a goat, a female without defect, for his sin which he has committed. He shall lay his hand on the head of the sin offering and slay the sin offering at the place of the burnt offering. The priest shall take some of its blood...Thus the priest shall make atonement for him, and he will be forgiven."

Notice that the first requirement for forgiveness of sins is met by a sacrifice without defect being offered and its blood being shed. The second requirement is met by the sinner laying his hand on the head of the offering. By doing this, he is repenting, by admitting he has sinned, and is identifying himself with the offering that is being sacrificed in his place for his sins.

Romans 6:23 proclaims, "the wages of sin is death." It is required by God's holy law that anyone who sins must die. 2 Chronicles 25:4 says, "every man shall die for his own sin" (WEB). Since, as Romans 3:23 states, "all have sinned," then it is required that all must die. However, through the offering of a sacrifice without defect on our behalf, the sacrifice dies in our place, its blood is shed, and upon repentance, our sins are forgiven.

In light of this second requirement of identification with the sacrifice as our sin bearer, what must we do to have our sins forgiven by virtue of the sacrifice that Jesus made for us by shedding His blood in His death on the cross? We must identify with Jesus by admitting that we have sinned, and by accepting Him as God's sacrifice for our sins. We do this by changing our minds, about our behavior and about who Jesus is.

In Acts 2:36-38, Peter was proclaiming the good news to the people in Jerusalem saying, "'Therefore let all the house of Israel know for certain that God has made Him both Lord and Christ—this Jesus whom you crucified.' Now when they heard *this*, they were pierced to the heart, and said to Peter and the rest of the apostles, 'Brethren, what shall we do?' Peter *said* to them, 'Repent, and each of you be baptized in the name of Jesus Christ for the forgiveness of your sins; and you will receive the gift of the Holy Spirit.'"

When we repent, we change our mind. We allow ourselves to be persuaded to believe that Jesus is the Christ, the Lord of all. By believing, we are laying our hand on Him and testifying that He died in our place and that we are placing our trust in the sacrifice that He made on our behalf. We identify with Jesus, confessing Him as Lord, and accepting His death for our sins. By believing and confessing, we identify with Jesus, testifying that He died in our place, and our sins are forgiven.

When we repent and believe, turning to Jesus we are transferred from darkness to light. Paul says in Acts 26:18 that Jesus sent him to the Gentiles "to open their eyes so that they may turn from darkness to light and from the dominion of Satan to God, that they may receive forgiveness of sins and an inheritance among those who have been sanctified by faith in Me." God's condition for our receiving His forgiveness is that we turn back to Him, that we turn from darkness to light.

God sent Jeremiah to warn His people about the disaster that He was going to bring upon them, in the hopes that, when they hear about it, "every man will turn from his evil way; then I will forgive their iniquity and their sin" (Jeremiah 36:3). This changing the mind about God and how we are living, and turning back to God, is a basic requirement for us to receive forgiveness of sins. I John 1:9 says: "If we confess our sins, He is faithful and righteous to forgive us our sins and to cleanse us from all unrighteousness."

This process is critically important to understand for our own salvation and for the edification or building up of the body of Christ, the church. Paul writes in Colossians 3:13, "bearing with one another, and forgiving each other, whoever has a complaint against anyone; just as the Lord forgave you, so also should you." To deal properly with our brothers and sisters in Christ, especially in the matter of forgiveness, it is necessary that we understand how the Lord has forgiven us. We are expected to forgive our brothers and sisters in Christ in the same way.

In Matthew 18:26-35, Jesus tells us a parable of a king and his servant. The servant owed a very large debt that he could not pay and begged for mercy and the king forgave his debt. The servant then went out and found a fellow servant that owed him a small debt and demanded payment. The fellow servant begged for mercy, but the servant would not listen and had him thrown into prison.

The other servants complained to the king. "Then summoning him, his lord said to him, 'You wicked slave, I forgave you all that debt because you pleaded with me. Should you not also have had mercy on your fellow slave, in the same way that I had mercy on you?' And his lord, moved with anger, handed him over to the torturers until he should repay all that was owed him. My heavenly Father will also do the same to you, if each of you does not forgive his brother from your heart."

Notice that the servant begged the king for mercy and was forgiven. The fellow servant begged that servant for mercy and was refused. This correlates to us repenting and receiving forgiveness from God, and then being unwilling to forgive someone that has repented of sinning against us.

Luke 17:3-4 warns: "Be on your guard! If your brother sins, rebuke him; and if he repents, forgive him. And if he sins against you seven times a day, and returns to you seven times, saying, 'I repent,' forgive him."

The principle is clear. To receive forgiveness, it is necessary that we repent, that we change our mind and think differently about what we have done and whether our behavior has been in accord with God's ways. If we have sinned and we realize the error of our way and change our mind about how we should live and act, and repent, God will forgive us. In the same way, if a brother or sister sins against us, and we rebuke them, and they see the error of their way and repent, then we must forgive them.

Matthew 6:14-15 says: "For if you forgive others for their transgressions, your heavenly Father will also forgive you. But if you do not forgive others, then your Father will not forgive your transgressions." Our responsibility is clear. We must forgive others just as the Lord has forgiven us. When our brother repents, we must forgive him.

There are some, who claim to be Christians, who believe you must forgive anyone for anything they do to you, whether or not they repent. However, we must not cheapen forgiveness. That would be the same as saying that because Jesus died for the sins of the world, everyone's sins are forgiven. We know from the Scriptures above that this is not true. Only those that have repented and believed in Jesus have forgiveness of sins.

Paul demonstrates the importance of not forgiving someone that has not seen the error of their way and has not repented. In 1 Corinthians 5:9-11, Paul instructs the believers concerning an unrepentant sinful brother. He writes: "I wrote you in my letter not to associate with immoral people; I *did* not at all *mean* with the immoral people of this world, or with the covetous and swindlers, or with idolaters, for then you would have to go out of the world. But actually, I wrote to you not to associate with any so-called brother if he is an immoral person, or covetous, or an idolater, or a reviler, or a drunkard, or a swindler—not even to eat with such a one." He says in verse five that we are to "deliver such a one to Satan for the destruction of his flesh, so that his spirit may be saved in the day of the Lord Jesus."

The idea of not even associating with a so-called believer that is living in sin is intended to bring about in that person a godly sorrow that leads to repentance. The sinning brother will thereby be encouraged to examine his behavior anew, and then, seeing the error of his way, he will be brought to godly sorrow and repentance.

The desire is that through this difficult and unpleasant way of dealing with a sinful brother, two things will be accomplished. One is that the brother will be restored to the Lord and to fellowship with all believers as soon as he repents.

The second and even more important purpose is to preserve the purity of the assembly. Paul says in 1 Corinthians 5:6, "Do you not know that a little leaven leavens the whole lump *of dough*?" And in verse thirteen he says, "Put away the wicked man from among yourselves" (WEB).

By failing to understand the basic principles of forgiveness, we jeopardize the eventual well-being of the sinning brother, and we compromise the purity of the assembly and the testimony of the Lord. Also, when we choose to do things according to our own understanding and not according to God's way and God's word, we are in rebellion and are jeopardizing our own relationship with the Lord and with His people.

However, when we are dealing with those outside of the church, with unbelievers, forgiveness has a whole different purpose. When an unbeliever sins against us we need to forgive them. Forgiving an unbeliever provides a testimony to them of God's unconditional love for all people. That testimony may be used by God to reach that unbeliever and eventually bring them to turn back to God.

Perhaps even more important is the effect it has on ourselves if we forgive the sinning unbeliever, regardless of whether they repent. This will protect our heart from becoming bitter (Hebrews 12:14-15). In order to prevent bitterness toward others, toward God, or even toward ourselves, and truly be able to forgive the sinning unbeliever from our heart, we must have a clear vision of God's sovereignty. We need to be convinced that God is in control, that things don't just happen.

When bad things happen, we need to understand that they would not have been able to happen unless God commanded or permitted them to happen. In Genesis chapter 45, Joseph's brothers, who had thrown him into a pit and sold him into slavery years earlier, had returned to Egypt because of the famine to buy food. They did not know that the one they had to deal with to buy the food was their brother Joseph.

In Genesis 45:7, Joseph reveals himself to his brothers and says, "It was not you who sent me here, but God." Joseph understood that no matter how bad the situation seemed that he found himself in, whether in a pit or in a prison, God was still in control and nothing could happen to him that God did not permit or cause.

In Job 1:6-2:7, we see that Satan had to get permission from God before he could do anything to afflict Job. Even after getting permission from God to afflict Job, Satan was specifically limited by God as to how far he could go in his affliction of Job.

If we are totally convinced that God is in control, that He is a good God, and that He wants only the best for us, then we can accept whatever happens in our lives as from His hand. With this attitude we will be able to forgive the people used by God to affect our lives.

We simply need to humble ourselves before the Lord and submit to Him and to His way. We need an ear to hear what the Spirit is speaking, and we need a heart to humbly and joyfully obey the Lord. When we do this, the Lord will be exalted.

The only way to healing and restoration is through humility, repentance, and forgiveness. This humbling is something that we each must choose to do. We must not wait for God to humble us. 1 Peter 5:6 exhorts: "Therefore humble yourselves under the mighty hand of God, that He may exalt you at the proper time, casting all your care upon Him, because He cares about you."

God allows trials and arranges circumstances to bring us to an end of our own strength, and to bring us to maturity in Christ. However, the decision to humble ourselves under His mighty hand must be our own. It must be our response to God working in our lives, believing that He loves us and desires the best for us.

With this attitude, we can joyfully submit to Him in the midst of any trial, forgiving, and not becoming bitter (James 1:2-4).

Chapter 9 Discussion Questions: Love and Forgiveness

1. How do we know that God's love is unconditional?
2. How do we know that God's forgiveness is not unconditional?
3. Why is it important that Jesus lived a sinless life?
4. How did Jesus pay the full price for our redemption?
5. What is required for the forgiveness of sins?
6. How did the Israelites identify with the offering being sacrificed for their sin?

7. How do we identify with Jesus as the sacrifice for our sins?

8. What does I John 1:9 say happens when a believer confesses their sins?

9. Why is it necessary to understand how God has forgiven us?

10. What happens if we refuse to forgive our brother or sister their transgressions?

11. What is the importance of not forgiving a believer that has not repented?

12. Why should we always forgive an unbeliever even if they do not repent?

God's Eternal
Purpose in Christ

W hat a glorious blessing to read through Ephesians chapters two and three as God reveals to us, through the apostle Paul, the mystery that has been hidden through the ages. This mystery was not made known to people of other generations, but it is now revealed to the apostles and prophets by His Spirit.

What is this mystery? It is that the Gentiles are co-heirs, members of the same body, and partners of the promise in Christ Jesus through the gospel. Paul was made a servant of this gospel to proclaim to the Gentiles the incalculable riches of Christ, and to shed light for all, about the administration of the mystery hidden for ages in God who created all things. But who are the Gentiles co-heirs with?

Ephesians 2:11-22 says, "Therefore remember that formerly you, the Gentiles in the flesh, who are called 'Uncircumcision' by the so-called 'Circumcision,' which is performed in the flesh by human hands— remember that you were at that time separate from Christ, excluded from the commonwealth of Israel, and strangers to the covenants of promise, having no hope and without God in the world. But now in Christ Jesus you who formerly were far off have been brought near by the blood of Christ.

"For He Himself is our peace, who made both groups into one and broke down the barrier of the dividing wall, by abolishing in His flesh the enmity, which is the Law of commandments contained in ordinances, so that in Himself He might make the two into one new man, thus establishing peace, and might reconcile them both in one body to God through the cross, by it having put to death the enmity. AND HE CAME AND PREACHED PEACE TO YOU WHO WERE FAR AWAY, AND PEACE TO THOSE WHO WERE NEAR; for through Him we both have our access in one Spirit to the Father.

"So then you are no longer strangers and aliens, but you are fellow citizens with the saints, and are of God's household, having been built on the foundation of the apostles and prophets, Christ Jesus Himself being the corner stone, in whom the whole building, being fitted together, is growing into a holy temple in the Lord, in whom you also are being built together into a dwelling of God in the Spirit."

How many times have we heard that Christ died on the cross to pay for our sins, and to reconcile us to God? Yet here Paul is not referring to Christ's death on the cross from the perspective of our individual reconciliation to God. Paul is revealing here a great mystery. This mystery is that Christ's death on the cross was to reconcile two groups into one by tearing down the dividing wall of hostility. Who are these two groups?

Paul refers here to the "circumcised" and the "uncircumcised." He refers to those that were of the citizenship of Israel and those "excluded" from the citizenship of Israel. Paul is speaking here of two groups, the Jews and the Gentiles.

Christ created in Himself one new man from the two. From the Jews and the Gentiles, Christ created in Himself one new man. He did this that He might reconcile both to God in one body through the cross and put the hostility between the two groups to death by it.

So now the Gentiles are no longer foreigners and strangers, but fellow citizens with the saints and members of God's household. Now the Jews and Gentiles are built together on the same foundation, the foundation of the apostles and the prophets, with Christ Jesus Himself as the cornerstone.

Paul continues in Ephesians 3:1-12, "For this reason I, Paul, the prisoner of Christ Jesus for the sake of you

Gentiles— if indeed you have heard of the stewardship of God's grace which was given to me for you; that by revelation there was made known to me the mystery, as I wrote before in brief. By referring to this, when you read you can understand my insight into the mystery of Christ, which in other generations was not made known to the sons of men, as it has now been revealed to His holy apostles and prophets in the Spirit; to be specific, that the Gentiles are fellow heirs and fellow members of the body, and fellow partakers of the promise in Christ Jesus through the gospel, of which I was made a minister, according to the gift of God's grace which was given to me according to the working of His power.

"To me, the very least of all saints, this grace was given, to preach to the Gentiles the unfathomable riches of Christ, and to bring to light what is the administration of the mystery which for ages has been hidden in God who created all things; so that the manifold wisdom of God might now be made known through the church to the rulers and the authorities in the heavenly places. This was in accordance with the eternal purpose which He carried out in Christ Jesus our Lord, in whom we have boldness and confident access through faith in Him."

At the very heart of this mystery is that the Gentiles are coheirs, members of the same body, and partners of the promise in Christ Jesus through the gospel. The Gentiles are co-heirs with whom? They are co-heirs with the Jews, with the children of Israel, with the sons of Abraham. The believing Gentiles are members of the same body as the believing Jews. These Gentiles are partners of the same promise in Christ Jesus through obedience to the gospel.

This is something that every believer, Jew and Gentile alike, needs to be keenly aware of. Jesus accomplished God's eternal purpose on the cross by making the two groups into one new man in Himself. God's eternal purpose is to have one body, prepared as a bride, without spot or wrinkle. It is for this bride that Christ is returning. God's eternal purpose is that of a loving father longing to have a spotless bride to present to His son. This is the ultimate expression of God's love.

Why is it so important for us to see and understand this mystery of the two being made one new man in Christ? This is critical because throughout the ages there has been an animosity, a hostility between the Jew and the Gentile. This is clearly manifested even in our day in the constant trouble in the Middle East. The world cannot have peace because of this hostility.

In the church, we can only have peace when we clearly understand that, by the blood of Christ, this hostility has been removed, and the dividing wall has been torn down. Whenever any believer is truly born again and the love of God is shed abroad in their heart, whether Jew or Gentile, this wall is torn down, and there is peace. By this, there is a deep realization of our oneness in Christ, which produces a genuine love for all the brothers, regardless of natural birth, regardless of whether they are Jews or Gentiles.

In Christ, we are all one. It is in this oneness that we are both reconciled to God. We are reconciled to God in one body through the cross. It is through the cross that this hostility has been put to death. When we died with Christ, the hostility between believers according to our flesh died also. It is by the death of this hostility that we are made one in Christ, resulting in peace.

When we see the necessity of this oneness between the Jewish believers and the Gentile believers for the accomplishment of God's eternal purpose, it is very troubling to hear so-called believers teach that there is a difference between the Jews and the Gentiles. Some teach that there are different rewards, different manifestations of the kingdom. Some teach that some Scriptures apply only to the Jews and that some Scriptures apply only to the Gentiles. Some have even divided the body based on whether the believer is by natural birth a Jew or a Gentile.

Perhaps they teach these destructive, divisive things because, being devoid of the Spirit, they can only see things according to the flesh. Having no understanding of spiritual things, they cannot understand the mysteries hidden for ages of God's eternal purpose in Christ. They see things according to physical descent and not according to faith.

Paul tells us clearly in Romans 2:28, "For a person is not a Jew who is one outwardly, and true circumcision is not something visible in the flesh. On the contrary, a person is a Jew who is one inwardly, and circumcision is of the heart— by the Spirit, not the letter. That man's praise is not from men but from God."

Paul continues to make this point in Galatians 3:6-9, "Just as Abraham believed God, and it was credited to him for righteousness, then understand that those who have faith are Abraham's sons. Now the Scripture saw in advance that God would justify the Gentiles by faith and told the good news ahead of time to Abraham, saying, 'All the nations will be blessed through you.' So those who have faith are blessed with Abraham, who had faith." Paul continues in verse 14, "The purpose was that the blessing of Abraham would come to the Gentiles by Christ Jesus, so that we could receive the promised Spirit through faith."

Paul continues this thought in verses 16-19, "Now the promises were spoken to Abraham and to his seed. He does not say "and to seeds," as though referring to many, but referring to one, and to your seed, who is Christ. And I say this: The law, which came 430 years later, does not revoke a covenant that was previously ratified by God and cancel the promise. For if the inheritance is from the law, it is no longer from the promise; but God granted it to Abraham through the promise. Why then was the law given? It was added because of transgressions until the Seed to whom the promise was made would come."

Paul concludes his thoughts in verses 22-29, "But the Scripture has imprisoned everything under sin's power, so that the promise by faith in Jesus Christ might be given to those who believe. Before this faith came, we were confined under the law, imprisoned until the coming faith was revealed. The law, then, was our guardian until Christ, so that we could be justified by faith. But since that faith has come, we are no longer under a guardian, for you are all sons of God through faith in Christ Jesus. For as many of you as have been baptized into Christ have put on Christ like a garment. There is no Jew or Greek, slave or free, male or female; for you are all one in Christ Jesus. And if you belong to Christ, then you are Abraham's seed, heirs according to the promise."

In Romans 9:6-8 Paul says, "But it is not as though the word of God has failed. For not all who are descended from Israel are Israel. Neither are they all children because they are Abraham's descendants. On the contrary, your offspring will be traced through Isaac. That is, it is not the children by physical descent who are God's children, but the children of the promise are considered to be the offspring."

In Romans 11:17-32 Paul continues, "Now if some of the branches were broken off, and you, though a wild olive branch, were grafted in among them and have come to share in the rich root of the cultivated olive tree, do not brag that you are better than those branches. But if you do brag— you do not sustain the root, but the root sustains you. Then you will say, 'Branches were broken off so that I might be grafted in.' True enough; they were broken off by unbelief, but you stand by faith. Do not be arrogant, but be afraid. For if God did not spare the natural branches, He will not spare you either.

"Therefore, consider God's kindness and severity: severity toward those who have fallen but God's kindness toward you—if you remain in His kindness. Otherwise you too will be cut off. And even they, if they do not remain in unbelief, will be grafted in, because God has the power to graft them in again. For if you were cut off from your native wild olive and against nature were grafted into a cultivated olive tree, how much more will these—the natural branches—be grafted into their own olive tree?

"So that you will not be conceited, brothers, I do not want you to be unaware of this mystery: A partial hardening has come to Israel until the full number of the Gentiles has come in. And in this way all Israel will be saved, as it is written: The Liberator will come from Zion; He will turn away godlessness from Jacob. And this will be My covenant with them when I take away their sins.

"Regarding the gospel, they are enemies for your advantage, but regarding election, they are loved because of the patriarchs, since God's gracious gifts and calling are irrevocable. As you once disobeyed God, but now have received mercy through their disobedience, so they too have now disobeyed, resulting in mercy to you, so that they also now may receive mercy. For God has imprisoned all in disobedience, so that He may have mercy on all."

From these passages it is clear that physical descent is meaningless. It is the spiritual reality that counts. It is not the children by physical descent who are God's children. Only the children of the promise are considered to be the offspring. Those who have faith, whether they are Jews or Gentiles, are truly Abraham's sons. It is only through disobedience and unbelief that any are cut off from the promise.

God has imprisoned all in disobedience that He may have mercy on all. That mercy, and the resulting sonship that is available to all, is only available by faith, by faith in Christ who is Abraham's seed. If you belong to Christ you are Abraham's seed, heirs according to the promise. In the end, all Israel will be saved, that is all that are of faith, all that are children of the promise, whether Jews or Gentiles. Only the unbelievers, whether Jews or Gentiles will perish and miss out on the blessings of the promise.

The writer of Hebrews says in Hebrews 10:29-31: "How much worse punishment do you think one will deserve who has trampled on the Son of God, regarded as profane the blood of the covenant by which he was sanctified, and insulted the Spirit of grace? For we know the One who has said, Vengeance belongs to Me, I will repay, and again, The Lord will judge His people. It is a terrifying thing to fall into the hands of the living God!" (HCSB).

It is not a small thing to build up what God in Christ has torn down, or to divide in two what God has made one. It is not a small thing to be found fighting against God and His eternal purpose. Colossians 3:11 assures us that "In Christ there is not Greek and Jew, circumcision and uncircumcision, barbarian, Scythian, slave and free; but Christ is all and in all" (HCSB).

John tells us in Revelation 21:1-4, "Then I saw a new heaven and a new earth, for the first heaven and the first earth had passed away, and the sea no longer existed. I also saw the Holy City, New Jerusalem, coming down out of heaven from God, prepared like a bride adorned for her husband. Then I heard a loud voice from the throne: Look! God's dwelling is with humanity, and He will live with them. They will be His people, and God Himself will be with them and be their God. He will wipe away every tear from their eyes. Death will no longer exist; grief, crying, and pain will exist no longer, because the previous things have passed away" (HCSB).

Again in verse nine John goes on to describe this holy city, the New Jerusalem saying, "Then one of the seven angels, who had held the seven bowls filled with the seven last plagues, came and spoke with me: 'Come, I will show you the bride, the wife of the Lamb.' He then carried me away in the Spirit to a great and high mountain and showed me the holy city, Jerusalem, coming down out of heaven from God, arrayed with God's glory.

"Her radiance was like a very precious stone, like a jasper stone, bright as crystal. The city had a massive high wall, with 12 gates. Twelve angels were at the gates; the names of the 12 tribes of Israel's sons were inscribed on the gates. There were three gates on the east, three gates on the north, three gates on the south, and three gates on the west. The city wall had 12 foundations, and the 12 names of the Lamb's 12 apostles were on the foundations" (HCSB).

Here at the very end of the Bible, at the end of the last book, we see the fulfillment of God's eternal purpose. Here we see the holy city, New Jerusalem, coming down out of heaven from God, prepared as a bride adorned for her husband. Here we see the bride spoken of in Ephesians chapter 5, without spot or wrinkle, holy and blameless, the wife of the Lamb.

Notice that in this description of the bride, the New Jerusalem, the names of the 12 tribes of Israel are inscribed on the gates. Notice also that the names of the Lamb's 12 apostles are on the foundations. Even in the final consummation of God's eternal purpose, the believing Jews and the believing Gentiles, the children of promise, the church, are forever together sharing the same destiny.

Revelation 22:3-5 reveals: "The throne of God and of the Lamb (Jesus) will be in it, and His bond-servants will serve Him; they will see His face, and His name will be on their foreheads. And there will no longer be any night; and they will not have need of the light of a lamp nor of the light of the sun, because the Lord God will illumine them; and they will reign forever and ever."

Let us heed the words of Paul in Ephesians 4:1-6: "Therefore I, the prisoner for the Lord, implore you to walk in a manner worthy of the calling with which you have been called, with all humility and gentleness, with patience, showing tolerance for one another in love, being diligent to preserve the unity of the Spirit in the bond of peace. There is one body and one Spirit, just as also you were called in one hope at your calling; one Lord, one faith, one baptism, one God and Father of all who is over all and through all and in all."

Chapter 10 Discussion Questions:
God's Eternal Purpose in Christ

1.   What is this mystery that has been hidden for ages?
2.   How is this mystery being revealed?
3.   Who are the circumcised and who are the uncircumcised?
4.   What was the purpose of Christ's death on the cross, beyond paying for our sins.
5.   What two groups did Christ reconcile to God in one body?
6.   Who are the Gentiles co-heirs with?
7.   How did Jesus accomplish God's eternal purpose?
8.   Why is it so important for us to see and understand this mystery?
9.   How has the hostility between the Jews and the Gentiles been put to death?
10. According to Galatians 3, who are Abraham's sons?
11. According to Romans 9, who are God's children?
12. Who has God imprisoned in disobedience that He might have mercy on them?

The Unity of the Spirit

B e "diligent to preserve the unity of the Spirit in the bond of peace." There are some very interesting observations that we can make concerning this brief passage from Ephesians 4:3, where Paul is writing to the believers in the church at Ephesus.

The first thing we notice in this passage is that these believers are admonished to keep or preserve something. This indicates that they, as genuine, born-again, Spirit-filled believers, had been given something, and that they were expected to keep it. In fact, it says that they are to be diligent, to make every effort, to keep it.

What they have been given, and were expected to make every effort to keep, was the unity of the Spirit. These Ephesians that had believed in Jesus, confessing Him to be Lord of all, had received the Holy Spirit and had been placed into the body of Christ by God.

Romans 12:4-5 says: "For just as we have many members in one body and all the members do not have the same function, so we, who are many, are one body in Christ, and individually members one of another." This body of Christ has many members, yet is one body. It was the Spirit that made the many into one body. This is the unity of the Spirit. This is the unity that they were instructed to make every effort to keep.

As believers, we do not need to try to become one body. We do not need to try to create a unity or oneness within the body of Christ. If we have been born of the Spirit, and the Spirit of Christ dwells in us, then we already have been given this unity. We only need to be concerned about keeping it, not about creating it. It is the Spirit that has made us one in Christ.

The next thing we notice is the way in which we are expected to attempt to keep this unity that has been given to us in the Spirit. We are to do it through the bond of peace. "Therefore I, the prisoner of the Lord, implore you to walk in a manner worthy of the calling with which you have been called, with all humility and gentleness, with patience, showing tolerance for one another in love, being diligent to preserve the unity of the Spirit in the bond of peace" (Ephesians 4:1-3).

What is this bond of peace? Ephesians 2:14 declares: "For He Himself is our peace, who made both *groups into* one and broke down the barrier of the dividing wall." Here we see that Christ is our peace. It is Christ that makes us one with God and one with one another. He removed the wall of hostility and set us at one, at peace with both God and man.

In John 14:27, Jesus tells His disciples: "Peace I leave with you; My peace I give to you; not as the world gives do I give to you. Do not let your heart be troubled, nor let it be fearful." The peace that Jesus had with the Father, He gives unto us. Jesus continues in John 16:33: "These things I have spoken to you, so that in Me you may have peace. In the world you have tribulation, but take courage; I have overcome the world."

This peace that Christ has given each believer is a peace that will never leave. In fact, because Christ is our peace, the peace He has given us is always there, fully available to us whenever we look to Him. Paul instructs us in Colossians 3:15: "Let the peace of Christ rule in your hearts, to which indeed you were called in one body; and be thankful." Paul goes on to say in Romans 14:19: "So then we pursue the things which make for peace and the building up of one another." We do this by allowing the peace of Christ to rule in our hearts. This ruling of Christ in our hearts as Lord is the bond of peace that keeps the unity of the Spirit.

We also see in Galatians 5:22-23 that "the fruit of the Spirit is love, joy, peace, patience, kindness, goodness, faithfulness, gentleness, self-control; against such things there is no law." When we are being led by the Spirit, this fruit of peace will be produced and manifested in our lives.

When we look at the context of Ephesians 4:3, we see this fruit of peace presented as the expectation of the kind of lives that we need to live in order to "keep" the unity of the Spirit. In Ephesians 4:1-6 Paul wrote, "I, the prisoner of the Lord, implore you to walk in a manner worthy of the calling with which you have been called, with all humility and gentleness, with patience, showing tolerance for one another in love, being diligent to preserve the unity of the Spirit in the bond of peace. *There is* one body and one Spirit, just as also you were called in one hope of your calling; one Lord, one faith, one baptism, one God and Father of all who is over all and through all and in all."

It becomes apparent that the way to keep the unity of the Spirit is to be led by the Spirit. All of the things that make for peace with God and with others are provided to us richly in the Spirit. All of these things, love, peace, forbearance, gentleness, humility, patience, produce an environment that enables us to be at peace. When we are walking by the Spirit, we will be making every effort to keep the unity of the Spirit. In fact, we can only keep the unity of the Spirit by walking in the Spirit.

It is the flesh that seeks to destroy this unity. Whenever we cease to be led by the Spirit, and begin to walk according to the flesh, this unity is damaged. Galatians 5:19-21 states: "Now the deeds of the flesh are obvious, which are: adultery, sexual immorality, uncleanness, lustfulness, idolatry, sorcery, hatred, strife, jealousies, outbursts of anger, rivalries, divisions, heresies, envy, murders, drunkenness, orgies, and things like these; of which I forewarn you, even as I also forewarned you, that those who practice such things will not inherit God's Kingdom."

The works of the flesh produce the very picture of the lack of peace: hatred, strife, jealousies, outbursts of anger, rivalries, divisions, heresies, envy, murders, drunkenness, and orgies. This is what is produced in our lives when we are not being led by the Spirit. Galatians 5:16-18 promises: "walk by the Spirit, and you won't fulfill the lust of the flesh. For the flesh lusts against the Spirit, and the Spirit against the flesh; and these are contrary to one another, that you may not do the things that you desire. But if you are led by the Spirit, you are not under the law" (WEB).

The flesh and the Spirit are contrary to each other. You cannot be led by the Spirit and gratify the desires of the flesh at the same time. You will either be walking by the Spirit and manifest the fruit of the Spirit, or you will be walking by the flesh and manifest the works of the flesh in your life. The flesh and the Spirit are mutually exclusive.

If you believe that you are walking by the Spirit, all you need to do is to take account of what is being produced in your life. Sit down and honestly take account of your actions, your words, and your thoughts. Consider what fruit is being produced in your life. Is it adultery, sexual immorality, uncleanness, lustfulness, idolatry, sorcery, hatred, strife, jealousies, outbursts of anger, rivalries, divisions, heresies, envy, murders, drunkenness, and orgies, or is it love, joy, peace, patience, kindness, goodness, faithfulness, gentleness, self-control?

It is important to realize that you can fool yourself all of the time. You can fool others some of the time. But you can never fool God. No matter how much you may try to hide it, God sees you as you really are. Paul writes in 2 Corinthians 5:9-11: "Therefore we also have as our ambition, whether at home or absent, to be pleasing to Him. For we must all appear before the judgment seat of Christ, so that each one may be recompensed for his deeds in the body, according to what he has done, whether good or bad. Therefore, knowing the fear of the Lord, we persuade men, but we are made manifest to God; and I hope that we are made manifest also in your consciences."

Many have wondered why there are so many divisions within the body of Christ. From the passages that we have considered already, it seems quite evident that some of these divisions are the result of the works of the flesh; hatred, discord, jealousy, fits of rage, selfish ambition, dissensions, factions and envy.

The believers in Corinth had divided into various groups claiming, "I am with Paul," or "I am with Apollos," or I am with Peter," or "I am with Christ." Paul says they are acting fleshly and not behaving as spiritual people. He urges these believers that there should be no divisions among them, that Christ is not divided.

We each must consider whether we are making every effort to keep the unity of the Spirit through the bond of peace, or are we trampling under foot the blood of the Son of God? Hebrew 10:29 warns: "How much severer punishment do you think he will deserve who has trampled under foot the Son of God, and has regarded as unclean the blood of the covenant by which he was sanctified, and has insulted the Spirit of grace?"

When we do not make every effort to keep the unity of the Spirit, we are insulting the Spirit of grace. When we choose our own way, when we place more importance on being right, than on being one in the Spirit, we are insulting the Spirit of grace. When we place more importance on the right position on minor issues and the right practices and rituals than we do on the oneness for which Christ died, then we are insulting the Spirit of grace.

Romans 12:18 exhorts: "If possible, so far as it depends on you, be at peace with all men." Romans 14:12-19 reminds: "So then each one of us will give an account of himself to God. Therefore let us not judge one another anymore, but rather determine this—not to put an obstacle or a stumbling block in a brother's way. I know and am convinced in the Lord Jesus that nothing is unclean in itself; but to him who thinks anything to be unclean, to him it is unclean. For if because of food your brother is hurt, you are no longer walking according to love.

"Do not destroy with your food him for whom Christ died. Therefore do not let what is for you a good thing be spoken of as evil; for the kingdom of God is not eating and drinking, but righteousness and peace and joy in the Holy Spirit. For he who in this *way* serves Christ is acceptable to God and approved by men. So then we pursue the things which make for peace and the building up of one another."

How important is it to you to make every effort to keep the unity of the Spirit through the bond of peace?

Chapter 11 Discussion Questions: The Unity of the Spirit

1. What did Paul encourage the believers at Ephesus to preserve?
2. Who placed the believers in Ephesus into the body of Christ?
3. Who made the many believers in Ephesus into one body?
4. What is the bond of peace?
5. How can we keep the unity of the Spirit?
6. What damages the unity of the Spirit?
7. How can we tell if we are walking by the Spirit?
8. Why are there so many divisions in the body of Christ?
9. When are we in danger of insulting the Spirit of grace?

Trusting the Holy Spirit

In order to trust the Holy Spirit, we must know and understand the Holy Spirit and how He works. The Scriptures clearly state that we are not to believe every spirit, but that we are to try the spirits to determine what source they are of (1 John 4:1).

To help us better understand the Holy Spirit and how He works, Paul sets forth in Galatians 5:19-21 a clear contrast between the Spirit and the flesh. The flesh, under the influence of the spirit of this world, the spirit of darkness, will lead us to exalt ourselves and to bring harm to the body of Christ and the glory of God. "Now the works of the flesh are obvious: sexual immorality, moral impurity, promiscuity, idolatry, sorcery, hatreds, strife, jealousy, outbursts of anger, selfish ambitions, dissensions, factions, envy, drunkenness, carousing, and anything similar, about which I tell you in advance – as I told you before – that those who practice such things will not inherit the kingdom of God" (HCSB).

The Holy Spirit which indwells every truly born-again believer will lead us to glorify God and to build up the body of Christ. In short, the Holy Spirit will lead us to love God and to love the brothers. Paul writes in Galatians 5:22-23 that "the fruit of the Spirit is love, joy, peace, patience, kindness, goodness, faithfulness, gentleness, self-control."

Romans 5:5 says, "the love of God has been poured out within our hearts through the Holy Spirit who was given to us." I Corinthians 13:4-8 speaks of this love of God that has been poured out in our hearts by the Holy Spirit. It says, "Love is patient, love is kind and is not jealous; love does not brag and is not arrogant, does not act unbecomingly; it does not seek its own, is not provoked, does not take into account a wrong suffered, does not rejoice in unrighteousness, but rejoices with the truth; bears all things, believes all things, hopes all things, endures all things. Love never fails."

In light of this contrast between the works of the flesh, under the leading of the spirit of this world, the spirit of darkness, and the fruit produced under the leading of the Holy Spirit, it is easy to discern or try the spirits. The enlightening of the eyes of our hearts by the working of the Holy Spirit within the believer enables us to clearly see the distinction and equips us with the understanding to be able to follow the Spirit's leading.

God has given us His Holy Spirit to equip us and to empower us to live holy lives in obedience to Him. His desire is that we would be holy as He is holy. His expectation is for every believer to walk as Jesus walked, in full and complete obedience to the will of the Father (I John 2:6). Peter tells us that God has given us everything necessary for life and godliness (2 Peter 1:3).

1 Thessalonians 4:3-8 exhorts us to walk in a way that is pleasing to God. Paul commands each believer to possess their own vessel in sanctification and honor, and not in lustful passions like those that do not know God. This is God's will for us, our sanctification, that we would be holy as He is holy. The salvation process that God is working out in the believer's life is being accomplished through sanctification by the Holy Spirit (2 Thessalonians 2:13).

In every aspect of our lives, God expects us to be holy, set apart for Him, for His glory. God is glorified when we walk in humble obedience to Him whether we are at home, at school, or at work. When we are led by the Holy Spirit, we are holy.

Galatians 5:16 says, "Walk by the Spirit and you will not carry out the desires of the flesh." Verses 24-25 continue, "Now those who belong to Christ Jesus have crucified the flesh with its passions and desires. If we live by the Spirit, let us also walk by the Spirit."

In order to be obedient to the Lord, we must hear Him. We must hear the leading of His Spirit. Many times, the Lord's speaking to us is very subtle. Many times, His speaking to us is as a still small voice. To hear His speaking, it is often necessary to be very focused on Him. We need an ear to hear, an ear tuned to the Lord. In order to obey, it is absolutely necessary to hear the Master's command.

This is not only true as we go through our daily lives out in the midst of the world. It is even more necessary when we gather together with other believers. Whether there are two or three of us or fifty-two or fifty-three of us, our purpose should be to glorify God and to build up the body of Christ.

We glorify God by obeying Him. We obey Him by following the leading of His Spirit. When we gather together with believers, the Spirit will give us the words to speak. He will put in our hearts what to say and when to say it. He will put in our hearts what songs to sing and when to sing them.

Ephesians 4:12-16 says the Lord gave some as gifts to the church "to prepare God's people for works of service, so that the body of Christ may be built up until we all reach unity in the faith and in the knowledge of the Son of God and become mature, attaining to the whole measure of the fullness of Christ.

"Then we will no longer be infants, tossed back and forth by the waves, and blown here and there by every wind of teaching and by the cunning and craftiness of men in their deceitful scheming. Instead, speaking the truth in love, we will in all things grow up into him who is the Head, that is, Christ. From him the whole body, joined and held together by every supporting ligament, grows and builds itself up in love, as each part does its work" (NIV).

In Ephesians 5:18-21, we are told to "be filled with the Spirit. Speak to one another with psalms, hymns and spiritual songs. Sing and make music in your heart to the Lord, always giving thanks to God the Father for everything, in the name of the Lord Jesus Christ. Submit to one another out of reverence for Christ" (NIV).

I Corinthians 14:26-33 says, "When you come together, everyone has a hymn, or a word of instruction, a revelation, a tongue or an interpretation. All of these must be done for the strengthening of the church. If anyone speaks in a tongue, two — or at the most three — should speak, one at a time, and someone must interpret. If there is no interpreter, the speaker should keep quiet in the church and speak to himself and God.

"Two or three prophets should speak, and the others should weigh carefully what is said. And if a revelation comes to someone who is sitting down, the first speaker should stop. For you can all prophesy in turn so that everyone may be instructed and encouraged. The spirits of prophets are subject to the prophets. For God is not a God of disorder but of peace" (NIV).

Each of these, the prophets and those sitting by, speak as the Spirit gives them utterance. Do we trust the Holy Spirit? Are we willing to, by faith, submit to His leading and to speak as He directs?

Jesus says in John 14:15-18, "If you love me, you will obey what I command. And I will ask the Father, and he will give you another Counselor to be with you forever— the Spirit of truth. The world cannot accept him, because it neither sees him or knows him. But you know him, for he lives with you and will be in you. I will not leave you as orphans; I will come to you" (NIV). It seems clear from this passage that this promised Spirit is Jesus Himself.

This is affirmed in 2 Corinthians 3:17-18, "Now the Lord is the Spirit, and where the Spirit of the Lord is, there is freedom. And we, who with unveiled faces all reflect the Lord's glory, are being transformed into his likeness with ever-increasing glory, which comes from the Lord, who is the Spirit" (NIV).

In Matthew 16:18 Jesus says, "I will build My church." We cannot, out of our own strength and natural abilities, build the church. Only Jesus can build the church. However, he builds his church by the leading and empowering of the Holy Spirit operating within each believer. As each believer humbly submits to the Lordship of Jesus, the Christ, in their lives and hears and obeys the leading of the Spirit, the church is built up.

God is a God of order, and by the leading of His Spirit, He will direct each member of the body of Christ concerning what to say and when to say it, and what to sing and when to sing it. In this way, God will be glorified, and the body of Christ will be built up by every joint of supply.

Ephesians 5:25-27 says, "Husbands, love your wives, just as also Christ loved the church and gave Himself for her, to make her holy, cleansing her in the washing of water by the word. He did this to present the church to Himself in splendor, without spot or wrinkle or any such thing, but holy and blameless" (HCSB).

Revelation 19:6-8 says, "Then I heard something like the voice of a vast multitude, like the sound of cascading waters, and like the rumbling of loud thunder, saying: Hallelujah – because our Lord God, the Almighty, has begun to reign! Let us be glad, rejoice, and give Him glory, because the marriage of the Lamb has come, and His wife has prepared herself. She was permitted to wear fine linen, bright and pure. For the fine linen represents the righteous acts of the saints."

Revelation 21:1-2 says, "Then I saw a new heaven and a new earth, for the first heaven and the first earth had passed away, and the sea existed no longer. I also saw the Holy City, new Jerusalem, coming down out of heaven from God, prepared like a bride adorned for her husband" (HCSB).

This is God's will for us, His purpose for us, that we would be built up together as Christ's body, the church, His bride. When Christ returns, He will be coming to receive His body, His bride. May we walk in humble obedience to the leading of the Holy Spirit that we may be blameless and holy, without spot or wrinkle, prepared for and eagerly awaiting the return of Jesus, the Christ, our Lord! Let us trust the Holy Spirit!

Chapter 12 Discussion Questions: Trusting the Holy Spirit

1. What is necessary in order for us to trust the Holy Spirit?
2. What does the indwelling Holy Spirit lead the believer to do?
3. What enables us to clearly see the distinction between the Holy Spirit and the spirit of this world?
4. Why has God given His Holy Spirit to us?
5. When are we holy?
6. What basic thing is necessary in order for us to obey the Lord?
7. How can we know what to speak and when to speak?
8. Why did God give some as gifts to the church?
9. How does the body build itself up in love?
10. How does Jesus build His church?
11. What is God's will for us?

Counterfeit Churches

T he church is an organism, a living body composed of the many people who have been born again by believing in, submitting to, and confessing the Lordship of Jesus, the Christ. The word church means the assembly of the called-out ones. This refers to the gathering together of those who have been born of the Spirit and called out of the world unto God.

These born-again, Spirit-filled Christians are all members of the body of Christ. This is one body with many members. This one body of Christ is expressed in every city or locality where these born-again believers assemble together, holding Christ alone as their head. The Scriptures refer to the church in Corinth, the church in Ephesus, the church in Laodicea, the churches of Judea, the churches of Asia, and the church that is in their house.

These called out ones look to Jesus to guide and direct them both individually, in their daily lives, and corporately, as they assemble together as the church, His living body. These Christians tolerate no one usurping the headship that is reserved only for their Lord, Jesus the Christ.

Colossians 2:18-19 warns us of those who would seek to defraud us of our prize in Christ being fleshly minded "and not holding fast the head, from which the entire body, being supplied and held together by the joints and ligaments, grows with a growth which is from God." It is essential, if the church is to be healthy and grow, it must hold fast to Christ as its head, diligently rejecting any and all who would seek to usurp Christ's place as the one and only head of the church.

Throughout His time on earth, Jesus continually taught His disciples. One of the lessons He stressed to them repeatedly was that of His unique place as head of the assembly, the church. He stressed that no one should exalt themselves over any other person in the church.

The day after Jesus and His disciples had come down from the Mount of Transfiguration, an argument started among the disciples as to who would be the greatest. Jesus, knowing the thoughts of their hearts, took a little child to Himself, and told His disciples: "For whoever is least among you – this one is great" (Luke 9:46-48, HCSB).

Then they left that place and made their way through Galilee and came to Capernaum. In the house at Capernaum, in response to another argument that had arisen among His disciples along the way concerning which of them was the greatest, Jesus said to them: "If anyone wants to be first, he must be last of all, and servant of all" (Mark 9:33-35, HCSB).

Again, while on their way up to Jerusalem, Jesus took His disciples aside privately and said to them; "You know that the rulers of the Gentiles dominate them, and the men of high position exercise authority over them. It must not be like that among you" (Matthew 20:25-26, HCSB).

And again, immediately after the "last supper," just before Jesus was arrested and crucified, He again admonished His disciples, sharing with them the thing that was most heavy upon His heart. Jesus said to them: "The kings of the Gentiles dominate them, and those who have authority over them are called 'Benefactors.' But it must not be like that among you. On the contrary, whoever is greatest among you must become like the youngest, and whoever leads, like the one serving" (Luke 22:25-26, HCSB).

Not only did Jesus stress this matter repeatedly to His disciples, He also confronted the religious leaders of His day concerning their arrogant ungodly behavior. Speaking to the crowds and to His disciples about the religious leaders in Matthew 23:2-13 Jesus said: "The scribes and the Pharisees have seated themselves in the chair of Moses; therefore all that they tell you, do and observe, but do not do according to their deeds; for they say *things* and do not do *them*. They tie up heavy burdens and lay them on men's shoulders, but they themselves are unwilling to move them with *so much as* a finger. But they do all their deeds to be noticed by men; for they broaden their phylacteries and lengthen the tassels *of their garments*.

"They love the place of honor at banquets and the chief seats in the synagogues, and respectful greetings in the market places, and being called Rabbi by men. But do not be called Rabbi; for One is your Teacher, and you are all brothers. Do not call *anyone* on earth your father; for One is your Father, He who is in heaven.

"Do not be called leaders; for One is your Leader, *that is*, Christ. But the greatest among you shall be your servant. Whoever exalts himself shall be humbled; and whoever humbles himself shall be exalted. But woe to you, scribes and Pharisees, hypocrites, because you shut off the kingdom of heaven from people; for you do not enter in yourselves, nor do you allow those who are entering to go in."

This is why these Christians, assembling together as the true church, tolerate no person usurping the headship that is reserved only for the Lord, Jesus the Christ. Jesus said in Matthew 18:20: "Where two or three are gathered together in my name, I am there among them." Christ leads during the assembly, and the believers follow (Hebrews 2:11-13). This body, thus, is living and vibrant, every member ministering one to another, freely giving and freely receiving from one another, as their Lord, Jesus, has freely given to them.

By this ministering of every member, this prophesying, this speaking the truth to one another in love, the body is built up, edified, made strong in the strength of the Lord by that which every joint supplies (1 Corinthians 14:26-33). Ephesians 4:15-16 says, "Speaking the truth in love, we are to grow up in all aspects into Him who is the head, even Christ, from whom the whole body, being fitted and held together by what every joint supplies, according to the proper working of each individual part, causes the growth of the body for the building up of itself in love." This is the church as seen in the Bible.

Some organizations that call themselves churches are really just a part of the world system. They are a part of the world's religious system of ceremonial worship. If they claim Christ as head, but in reality their head is man himself, they are counterfeit churches. If they are devoid of the Spirit of God, but are full of the spirit of this world, they are counterfeit churches. If they only give lip service to the Scriptures, but embrace the philosophy and doctrines of men, they are counterfeit churches.

Counterfeit churches have existed since the time of the first century church. The apostle John writes in 2 John 7, "For many deceivers have gone out into the world, those who do not acknowledge Jesus Christ as coming in the flesh. This is the deceiver, the antichrist." John refers to one of these antichrists by name in 3 John 9-10, "I wrote something to the church; but Diotrephes, who loves to be first among them, does not accept what we say. For this reason, if I come, I will call attention to his deeds which he does, unjustly accusing us with wicked words; and not satisfied with this, he himself does not receive the brethren, either, and he forbids those who desire to do so and puts them out of the church."

These antichrists are deceivers and false teachers. They do not acknowledge that Jesus Christ, as the life-giving Spirit, is dwelling in born-again believers. They do not acknowledge Jesus Christ as coming in the flesh. Their counterfeit churches refuse to receive the true brothers and put genuine believers out of the church. This reminds me of the passage in Matthew 9:17, "Nor do people put new wine into old wineskins; otherwise the wineskins burst, and the wine pours out and the wineskins are ruined; but they put new wine into fresh wineskins, and both are preserved."

It seems that when someone in a counterfeit church gets saved, eventually the antichrists that run the church will have the true believer thrown out. When the antichrists become aware of the Spirit of God bubbling up and overflowing in the believer, they realize that, to protect their kingdom, they have to eliminate the source of effervescence or it will eventually burst open their old wineskin.

If the believer chooses to remain there, the bubbling up of the Spirit will eventually be quenched and he will begin to lose his passion for the Lord and will begin to conform to the will of the antichrists. New wine must be put into new wineskins. Spirit filled believers are not compatible with counterfeit churches. Spirit filled believers must be put into genuine churches, then both the believer and the church will grow and mature together.

Are you a member of the body of Christ, the church, or are you simply a member of a religious organization, a counterfeit church? The meetings you attend, are they conducted according to the pattern set forth clearly in Scripture, where Christ alone is the head, or are they conducted, controlled, planned, and directed by a person, or persons, who have usurped the headship of Christ?

Perhaps you find yourself in the dilemma of being new wine in an old wineskin. Perhaps you are a member of the body of Christ but are assembling together with an organization that is just a part of the worldly religious system, a counterfeit church. Perhaps you attend the meetings of that organization because it gives you a sense of righteousness, because by just being there, you have, in some way, done your religious duty. Yet, there is still within you such a sense of frustration and emptiness because, deep inside, you know that there must be something more. The Spirit bubbling up within you tells you there must be something more.

You long to be fed. You long even more to be able to feed others, to share with the body that which your Lord has given so freely to you, yet there is no opportunity. The system prohibits it. The system holds you in bondage by its traditions, teachings, and practices. It holds out a promise of satisfaction, but never the fulfillment. Perhaps it even tells you that if you leave, you will be lost and will go to hell.

This world's religious system's one purpose is to keep you from ever experiencing the real church, the unity of the Spirit and the oneness of the body of Christ, holding fast Christ as head. The counterfeit churches are a part of this world, this world that lies in the evil one. This religious system of counterfeit churches is the world's great secret weapon.

In the real church, the apostles, prophets, evangelists, shepherds, and teachers are given as gifts for the training, the equipping of the saints. The saints then are to do the work of the ministry, the work of building up the church. The saints are being trained to lift up Jesus, speaking forth Christ, both in the meetings and in their daily lives.

The trainers are training the saints to know the indwelling Holy Spirit and to hear His voice. The saints need to be trained to listen to the Spirit's speaking and to be diligent to obey. This training is to continue until we all arrive at the unity of the faith and maturity in Christ. The saints are to be trained to know and use the gifts of the Holy Spirit to serve one another and to build up the church, the body of Christ.

"My people did not listen to My voice, And Israel did not obey Me. So I gave them over to the stubbornness of their heart, to walk in their own devices. Oh that My people would listen to Me, that Israel would walk in My ways! I would quickly subdue their enemies and turn My hand against their adversaries. Those who hate the LORD would pretend obedience to Him" (Psalm 81:11-15).

Pretending to be the church, these counterfeit churches are used by the world to keep the genuine church, the body of Christ, from being built up. Christ died to make us one body with Himself as head. However, these man-made counterfeit churches have divided the body of Christ into many parts and have built massive walls between the various camps to keep them separated, and sometimes to keep them fighting each other. They have usurped the place of Christ as head of the church.

Are you in a counterfeit church? Is God calling you to come out of it and be separate from it and begin to assemble together with other believers as the true church, the body of Christ, that recognizes no head but Christ Himself? The real church is composed of born-again believers that have been called to come out of the world system unto God.

If you believe that God raised Jesus from the dead, and have confessed Him as Lord, don't you desire to live according to His Lordship in your meeting life as well as in your daily life? Jesus died for our sins that we might be delivered from this present evil world, delivered from its religious systems, and be brought into the fullness of His kingdom in the church.

Here in the church, while holding Christ as head, we each have every opportunity and responsibility to minister to, and receive from, one another, as Christ directs. We do this by esteeming each other as better than ourselves, that through every joint of supply, the body might build itself up in love.

This is what Christ is longing for. He desires a body, built up and mature, as a bride prepared for His return, looking to Him alone as its head.

Chapter 13 Discussion Questions: Counterfeit Churches

1. What is the meaning of the term "church" as used in Scripture?
2. Who is the head of this church?
3. What lesson did Jesus stress repeatedly to His disciples?
4. When two or more believers are gathered together, who leads the assembly?

5. How are we to grow up in all aspects into Him who is the head?

6. What is a counterfeit church?

7. Who is head of the counterfeit churches?

8. What happens if someone in a counterfeit church gets saved?

9. What happens if you put new wine into old wineskins?

10. What is the source of the effervescence that endangers the counterfeit church?

11. Who are the trainers in the church?

12. What are they training the saints to do?

The Antichrists

~~~~

The term "antichrist" or "antichrists" appears five times in Scripture. All of these are found in the epistles of John. It appears four times in the first and once in the second epistle.

Let us begin by examining the meaning of the word in the original Greek, and then look at how it is used by the apostle John in his writings. The Greek word is "antichristos." This is made up of two Greek words, "anti" which means instead of, as a substitute for, or something in place of something else, and "christos" which means Messiah or Christ. John uses the term antichristos or antichrist to refer to someone or something that is "instead of" or "in place of" or substituted for the Christ. The Christ referred to here is Jesus, the Christ, our Lord.

Now, let us examine the context of the passages where John uses this term. I John 2:18 says, "It is the last hour; and just as you heard that antichrist is coming." John speaks of an antichrist that is coming, referring to that spoken of by the Lord in Matthew 24:15, where He quotes from Daniel 11:31. In the same verse, however, John speaks of antichrists, plural, that had already appeared. He says, "Even now many antichrists have appeared; from this we know that it is the last hour."

John is speaking here of two different things. The first is the antichrist that, at the end times, will set himself up as Christ and attempt to have all people worship him. The second, the antichrists, refers to those that were among the Christians and had attempted to set themselves up as being above the common believers, in place of Christ. It is this group of people, these antichrists upon which we want to focus. Here we see them going out and teaching their rebellious ideas, having been rejected by the church.

In 1 John 4:1-3, John exhorts the Christians to "not believe every spirit, but test the spirits to see whether they are from God, because many false prophets have gone out into the world." He says that these false prophets that have gone out have the spirit of antichrist "which you have heard that it is coming, and now it is already in the world." Again, John indicates that these antichrists exist and are already in the world.

This leads us to Revelation 2:6, where the Lord writes to the church at Ephesus, which many believe represents the early first century church. He says to it: "Yet this you do have, that you hate the deeds of the Nicolaitans, which I also hate."

The Greek word translated Nicolaitans comes from two Greek words. The first is 'nikos' which means conquest or conquerors. The second is 'laos' which means the people. The Nicolaitans were conquerors of the people.

They were those in the first century church that were attempting to set themselves apart from and above the rest of the believers as a special class. Just as we saw in I John, these conquerors of the people, not being accepted by the church and allowed to carry out this divisive practice, went out into the world, with this spirit of antichrist, spreading their false teaching.

Jude writes in his letter to the believers, urging the brothers to contend earnestly for the faith. "Contend" here means to enter into an arena and do battle publicly, fighting whole-heartedly for the faith.

Certain persons had crept in unnoticed into the fellowship of the believers, denying the Lordship of our Master and Lord, Jesus Christ, setting themselves up above and apart from the other believers, in the place reserved for Christ alone. Jude charges the believers to withstand them openly. The brothers were urged to do battle with them publicly and not to sit idly by and allow these persons to steal away the faith once delivered to the saints.

In verse 11 Jude refers to these people as having "gone the way of Cain, and for pay they have rushed headlong into the error of Balaam, and perished in the rebellion of Korah." The "way of Cain" refers to Genesis chapter 4 where Cain attempts to worship God in his own way, disregarding the way that God had set forth. These false teachers set up their own form of worship, focused on the leadership of man, rather than the Lordship of Christ.

The "error of Balaam" refers to Numbers 22:1-25:9, where Balaam, because of his love for honor and money, was willing to go, contrary to God's instruction, to the high places of Baal and prophecy. It was because of Balaam's counsel that the daughters of Midian were able to cause the sons of Israel to defect from the Lord (Numbers 31:16). In the same way, these false teachers Jude refers to are flattering people for their own advantage because they love money and honor. For pay, they pretend to serve God, while actually causing the children of God to defect from Him, just as Balaam did.

The "rebellion of Korah" refers to Numbers 16 where Korah and all his company spurned the Lord and His authority, Moses and Aaron. They felt that they were naturally qualified to lead the people and minister to the Lord. Jude identifies these false teachers as "mockers, following after their own ungodly lusts. These are the ones who cause divisions, worldly-minded, devoid of the spirit" (Jude 1:18-19).

These are the ones that despise God's authority, Jesus Christ, the head of the body. They are willing to divide the body of Christ, so they might have their own little kingdom to rule over. Their desire for power is so great that they care more for that, than for the oneness of the body for which Christ died.

These false teachers, that Jude urges the brothers to contend with, are those that have crept into the church unnoticed. They have turned the grace of God into an opportunity to fulfill the lusts of the flesh, lusting after position, honor, money, and power. They speak arrogantly, flattering people, in order to gain an advantage over them. They are willing to do anything in order to have a little kingdom of their own, even to the destruction of the body of Christ.

Now we must go back to the book of Revelation 2:14-15, where the Lord is writing to the church in Pergamum. He says he has a few things against them because they "have some who hold the teaching of Balaam" and some "who in the same way hold the teaching of the Nicolaitans." These teachings had come into the church and were in danger of being accepted by the church.

The Lord commands the church to repent, lest He come and make war against them. Here we have people in the church who have not only come into the church and begun the practice of taking money for the service they perform and setting themselves up apart from the common people in the church as a special class, but they have begun teaching this apostasy in the church as accepted doctrine.

Thus the clergy system is fully born, and the apostasy of the church is assured, for the people in the church have begun to accept man as their head, instead of, or in place of, Christ. Now the antichrists have not just gone out from the church, as John had warned, but now they have crept back into the church and set themselves up in the church. They have done this because, as Jude says, they are "devoid of the spirit."

They have no confidence in Christ being able to govern the church by means of His Spirit leading and directing each member of the body. Rather, their confidence is in the flesh, in the ability of man to govern, guide, direct and control the church of God, especially through them. They have replaced Christ as the head of the church here on earth. They have a form of godliness but deny the power thereof. Paul tells Timothy to avoid such men (2 Timothy 3:1-7). Instead of focusing on being followers of Christ, they focus on being leaders of men.

Taking the place of Christ as head of the church is an extremely serious matter. In Luke 22:24-27, after breaking the bread and drinking the wine of the last supper with His disciples, Jesus spoke to them of this very thing. A dispute arose among the disciples as to which of them would be greatest. The Lord rebuked them saying that the rulers of the Gentiles lord it over their subjects, but with the disciples it must not be so. Rather, the greatest was to be as if he were the youngest, and the leader, as a servant, as the least or the lowest.

What is the situation today? Certain people have set themselves up as separate, apart from, and above, the common people in some churches to rule over them? They have taken the place of Christ, ruling by their own authority, controlling, manipulating, directing, and lording it over the common believers? Jeremiah 5:31 records these words: "The prophets prophesy falsely, and the priests rule by their own authority; and My people love to have it so!" How long will these churches tolerate these antichrists in their midst? How long until these simple believers of our Lord say, "Enough, we want no king but Jesus!"?

Let us go back to the book of 1 Samuel chapter 8, where, in verse 5, the children of Israel came to Samuel saying: "We want a king over us just like the nations." Samuel was offended and went to God. God told Samuel in verse 7: "Listen to the people because they have not rejected you, but they have rejected me from being king over them." God then told Samuel to go to the people and tell them what this king would do to them when he would rule over them.

This king would take their sons and daughters and place them for himself in his chariots and among his horsemen and they will run before his chariots. They will do his plowing and harvesting and make his weapons of war. They will make perfume for him, cook and bake for him. He will take the best of their fields, vineyards and seed, and give them to his servants. He will take their servants and use them for his work. He will take the best of their flocks and they themselves will become his servants. Then the Lord said to the children of Israel in 1 Samuel 8:18: "*Then* you will cry out in that day because of the king you have taken for yourselves, but the Lord will not answer you in that day."

God is calling for His people to come out of the apostate, fallen, worldly religious system. He is calling them to come unto Himself and be separate, and be His people, ruled over by His king, Jesus, the Christ, our Lord.

As we come to the King of kings and Lord of lords, let us come as those esteeming one another as better than ourselves, submitting ourselves joyfully to one another, not any lording it over another. May we be those that hold fast the Head, Jesus our Lord, alone (Colossians 2:18-19).

Chapter 14 Discussion Questions:
The Antichrists

1. What does the word antichrist mean?
2. What are the two types of antichrist referred to in the epistles of John?
3. When will each of these types appear?
4. What two Greek words does the word Nicolaitans come from?
5. What do those two words mean?
6. What does the 'Way of Cain' refer to?
7. What does the 'Error of Balaam' refer to?
8. What does the 'Rebellion of Korah' refer to?
9. What does Jude say that the false teachers had done?
10. What does Jesus have against the church in Pergamum?
11. What did God tell Samuel that the king would do when he would rule over them?
12. What did God say the people's response to the king's rule would be?

Come Out of Her, My People

E veryone likes a good mystery. Some of the greatest mysteries in the world are found in the last book of the Bible, the book of Revelation. Perhaps the greatest of these mysteries is found in the book of Revelation, chapters 17 and 18.

Most mysteries are intended for relaxation and enjoyment, but this mystery is presented as a warning. It is a warning with some very dire consequences for those that do not understand it and heed it. Failure to obey its warning will have the most serious results.

In chapter 17, John, the apostle, is shown a vision of a woman. In verse 5 we see that: "on her forehead was a name written, a mystery, 'BABYLON THE GREAT, THE MOTHER OF HARLOTS AND OF THE ABOMINATIONS OF THE EARTH.'"

Who or what is this mystery? What does she represent? And most of all, why is this mystery of any importance to us?

Before we begin to consider who or what this woman represents, let's lay the groundwork for this discussion by examining why understanding this mystery is so important. To do this, we need to turn to chapter 18 of the book of Revelation and look at verse 2.

Here an angel has come down from heaven and is crying out saying: "Fallen, fallen is Babylon the Great!" You might have noticed that this is the same name as appeared on the woman's forehead, "Babylon the Great." So, we see that this is the same woman of mystery from chapter 17.

This declaration is immediately followed by a warning, in verse 4, from: "another voice from heaven, saying, 'Come out of her my people, that you will not participate in her sins and receive of her plagues.'" Whatever is represented by "Babylon the Great," God clearly and solemnly warns his people to come out of her.

Here lies the importance of understanding this mystery. God's warning here is to His people. He is warning them of the urgent necessity for all of them to come out of this "Babylon the Great" lest they be judged with her and suffer the plagues that He is about to bring upon her.

The problem is that unless we, as God's people, understand what is meant by this mysterious woman, "Babylon the Great," we will not know how to come out of her. How can we obey Him and be saved from her plagues if we don't know who she is? It is essential, therefore, that we gain an understanding of the meaning of this "mystery."

Let's begin our quest for understanding of this mystery by returning to chapter 17, verse 1 of the book of Revelation. Here we see this woman described as "the great harlot who sits on many waters." Verse 15 says, "The waters which you saw where the harlot sits, are peoples and multitudes and nations and tongues." This woman's presence is evidently spread throughout the whole earth.

Verse 3 describes this woman as: "sitting on a scarlet beast, full of blasphemous names, having seven heads and ten horns." Then verse 4 says: "The woman was clothed in purple and scarlet, and adorned with gold and precious stones and pearls, having in her hand a gold cup full of abominations and of the unclean things of her immorality."

This sounds almost impossible to understand, a harlot riding on a beast that has seven heads and ten horns. How can anyone understand what this strange picture represents? Yet, we know that God wants us to understand it, because He says in verse seven: "I will tell you the mystery of the woman, and of the beast that carries her, which has the seven heads and the ten horns."

121

We need to be encouraged by this, knowing that God wants us to understand the mystery. In fact, to be obedient to Him, we must understand this mystery.

In verses 8-18, the angel explains the meaning of each of these things. The seven heads are seven mountains. These mountains represent seven kings. The beast was one of these seven, and is not, and will be the eighth, and will go into destruction. The ten horns are ten kings that will receive power for one hour with the beast. These ten kings will hate the woman and attack her and destroy her because God will put it in their heart to do it. Then the ten kings will give their authority to the beast until the words of God should be fulfilled. The woman is that great city or community that rules over the kings of the earth.

The Greek word "polis" is usually translated as city. However, then verse 18 would be translated, "The woman that you saw is the great city that rules over the kings of the earth." Many have used this translation to conclude that the woman is Rome, because of the power that it wields over the kings of the earth via the Catholic church. However, the Catholic church has little or no influence over the vast majority of the world that is not Catholic, and especially not Christian. Rome has virtually no influence over the Muslims, the Hindus, the Buddhists, and so on.

Being there is no individual city that I am aware of that rules over the kings of the earth, I have chosen to accept an alternate but very similar meaning of "polis." I have chosen to consider that the woman represents some sort of community that rules over the kings of the earth, rather than a particular city. Then verse 18 would be translated, "The woman that you saw is that great community that rules over the kings of the earth."

We need to seek God for understanding, that we might come to know the identity of this great community that is represented by this woman of mystery. This is a community that has ruled over the kings of the earth throughout the ages. Yet, in the last days this community will be destroyed by the ten kings, who will give their authority over to the beast. Identifying this community is essential, because if we cannot identify it, we cannot come out of it as God has commanded us to do.

In solving a mystery, the trick is to discern between the clues that lead to a proper conclusion based on the facts, and those that simply distract our focus from our objective. Remember, our objective is to determine the identity of the woman who has been referred to as "Babylon the Great" and the community that she represents.

Down through the ages, much time and effort have been spent trying to determine what the beast, the seven heads and the ten horns mean. I believe that consideration of these clues may simply prove to be a distraction from our objective. Instead of following these clues, let's attempt to determine the identity of this woman of mystery, Babylon the Great, by examining what Babylon represented in the Scriptures of the Old Testament.

Let us begin this examination by going back to the first time this word Babylon is used in the Hebrew Scriptures. We can start by looking up the word "Babylon" in *Strong's Exhaustive Concordance*. Here we learn that the Hebrew word is Babel, the same word used in Genesis 10:10 and 11:9, which means "confusion." This refers to the confusion that resulted from a group of people that came together, as recorded in Genesis chapter 11, with a desire to make a name for themselves. To accomplish this, these people began to build a city with a great tower reaching up to heaven.

This is reminiscent of Cain in Genesis 4, where he desired to worship God in his own way. His efforts were rejected by God and resulted in the murder of his brother. Cain then goes on to build a city that he names after his son, Enoch. This was the result of an individual refusing to worship God in God's way.

In chapter 11 we see the result of a corporate refusal to worship God in God's way, again culminating in the building of a city with its high tower, with the expressed purpose of reaching up to heaven by their own effort, in their own way. The result of this idolatrous activity was confusion, as God came in and judged their rebellious activity and confounded their languages.

The people were scattered from Babel to the far corners of the earth. Along with them they took this idolatrous spirit that has resulted in every culture developing their own religious system in which they worship God, or gods, in whichever way seems right in their own eyes. It could be said, therefore, that Babel, or Babylon, had become the mother of all the idolatrous cities of the earth.

Both the Greek and the Hebrew words translated as "harlot" also mean idolatry. So, it becomes clear that what is being referred to in each case here is idolatry, the worship of pagan gods or the worship of God in the way in which pagans worship.

God speaks to His people in Deuteronomy 12:1-2 saying: "These are the statutes and the judgments which you shall carefully observe in the land which the Lord, the God of your fathers, has given you to possess as long as you live on the earth. You shall utterly destroy all the places where the nations whom you shall dispossess serve their gods, on the high mountains and on the hills and under every green tree."

In verse 4, He continues saying: "You shall not act like this toward the Lord your God. But you shall seek the Lord at the place which the Lord your God will choose from all your tribes, to establish His name there for His dwelling, and there you shall come." Then in verse 8: "You shall not do at all what we are doing here today, every man doing whatever is right in his own eyes." And in verse 13: "Be careful you do not offer your burnt offering in every place you see."

Clearly, what is referred to by the word "harlot" in Isaiah chapter 1, Jeremiah chapter 2 and 3, and Ezekiel chapter 16, when referring to Jerusalem and Israel, is idolatry. "Babylon the Great" is the mother of idolatry and of the idols of the world. It becomes obvious that the great community it represents is the religious community to which all the kings of the earth must pay homage. No king can long rule his people unless he embraces their religion.

Revelation 14:6-7 speaks of another angel flying in mid heaven with a gospel to preach to the whole earth proclaiming: "Fear God, and give Him glory." Then, in verse 8, a second angel declares: "Fallen, fallen is Babylon the great." Here we have one angel preaching the gospel to fear God and worship him and a second angel announcing the end of the world's idolatrous religious system, the religious Babylon.

This is followed by a third angel, in verses 9-12, warning about an even more dangerous and idolatrous system of worship about to be established by the beast, the forced worship of himself. This will take place after the ten kings have destroyed the world's religious systems, the woman, "Babylon the Great." Only after all religions are eliminated will the people be willing to worship the beast.

God is calling His people to come out of the worldly, man-made, religious system, before His judgment falls upon them. He is calling His people to come out of all that is contrary to His pattern of worship found in the Scriptures.

God will not tolerate His people worshipping Him in every high place that they choose. He wants us to come out of the world's religious system and separate ourselves unto Him. He wants His people to worship Him in His way, in His place, according to His pattern. We must obey and come out or we will receive the plagues with which he judges the Harlot, Babylon the Great!

"God is spirit, and those who worship Him must worship in spirit and in truth" (John 4:24). This is the worship God wants, not worship in the shadowy emptiness of religious practice. We must worship in spirit and reality. We must hold fast to Christ as our head.

Christ must be our Lord and our life. We must flee the emptiness of religion and enter into the fullness of Christ. "For the entire fullness of God's nature dwells bodily in Christ, and you have been filled by Him, who is the head over every ruler and authority" (Colossians 2:9-10).

My prayer is that all who know Jesus as Lord will have an ear to hear, and a heart to obey!

Chapter 15 Discussion Questions: Come Out of Her, My People

1. What is the purpose of this mystery?
2. What is the warning issued in Revelation 18:4?
3. Why is it important to learn the identity of the woman referred to as "Babylon the Great"?
4. How do we know that God wants us to understand this mystery?
5. What does Revelation 17:18 say that the woman represents?
6. Where is the first time that the word Babylon is used in Scripture?
7. What does God say in Deuteronomy 12:1-2 that the Israelites must do when they enter the promised land?
8. What does God tell them in Deuteronomy 12:8?
9. What great community does the woman represent that all the kings of the earth must pay homage to?
10. What does it say that the 10 kings will do to the woman?
11. What system of worship is forced after the woman is destroyed?
12. What worship does God require from those that worship Him?

Life after Death

S ome people believe that there is no life after death. They believe that when you die it is all over–no heaven, no hell, and no judgment. Others believe that there is a final judgment where believers will go to heaven and receive a reward and unbelievers will be sentenced to an eternity of torment in hell.

Our goal in this study is to determine, from the divinely-inspired words of Scripture, what God has revealed concerning life after death, concerning any judgment that may await us, and concerning how to prepare for that coming judgment. Knowledge is power. An understanding of what, if anything, awaits us after we die will help to equip us to be prepared for it.

With this knowledge, this understanding of what awaits us after death, we will be given the opportunity to be prepared for the coming judgment and to confront it with boldness and confidence. This coming judgment need not be a time of fear and dread. In this study, we shall see that if we are properly prepared, this coming judgment will be a time of rejoicing!

The place commonly referred to as "hell" seems central to any concept of life after death and any coming judgment. Therefore, we will begin our study by attempting to get a better understanding of what is meant by this word "hell."

Using *Strong's Concordance* we find that the word "hell" appears 23 times in the King James Version of the New Testament. However, these 23 passages have translated three different Greek words into the one English word "hell."

"Hades" is translated as hell 10 times, "Gehenna" is translated as hell 12 times, and "Tartarus" once. This has resulted in a great deal of confusion about hell. To clear up some of this confusion, we need to understand what is meant by each of these three Greek words that have been translated as hell.

We will begin by using the New American Standard Bible (NASB) to examine how the word "Hades" is used in Scripture. In Acts 2:27 Peter quotes King David's prophecy that God will not leave the soul of Jesus in Hades saying, "You will not abandon my soul to Hades." David's words here are taken directly from Psalm 16:10 where it says, "You will not abandon my soul to Sheol." Here the Hebrew word translated as "hell" in the King James Version of the Old Testament is actually "Sheol."

This passage proves that Sheol in Hebrew and Hades in Greek are names for the same place. Secondly, this passage states that Hades or Sheol is the place where the souls of people go when their body dies, just as it was prophesied about Jesus' soul.

Some people believe that when a Christian dies, that person then goes immediately to heaven to be with the Lord forever. They use the verse in Philippians 1:23 where Paul says that he has the "desire to depart and be with Christ." This interpretation sounds appealing, no accountability, no judgment, just go directly to heaven–but it is not consistent with what the Scriptures teach.

First of all, to go to be with the Lord does not necessarily mean to go to heaven. Psalm 139:7-8 says, "Where can I go from Your Spirit? Or where can I flee from Your presence? If I ascend to heaven, you are there; if I make my bed in Sheol, behold, You are there."

Secondly, 1 Thessalonians 4:13-18 says, "But we do not want you to be uninformed, brethren, about those who are asleep, so that you will not grieve as do the rest who have no hope. For if we believe that Jesus died and rose again, even so God will bring with Him those who have fallen asleep in Jesus. For this we say to you by the word of the Lord, that we who are alive and remain until the coming of the Lord, will not precede those who have fallen asleep (died). For the Lord Himself will descend from heaven with a shout, and with the voice of the archangel and with the trumpet of God, and the dead in Christ will rise first. Then we who are alive and remain will be caught up together with them in the clouds to meet the Lord in the air, and so we shall always be with the Lord. Therefore comfort one another with these words."

This passage clearly states that those Christians that have died, fallen asleep, before Christ's return, have not gone up to heaven. Rather, it says that Christ will descend from heaven with a shout and with the trumpet of God, and that these dead in Christ will rise to meet Him first, then those Christians that are still alive at His coming will be caught up together with them to meet the Lord in the air.

When believers die their souls go down to Hades, just as Jesus' did. They do not rise until Christ's return. When Jesus returns, the souls of the believers will rise to meet the Lord in the air, first the dead in Christ, then those who are still alive at His coming.

In Luke 16:19-31 Jesus says, "Now there was a rich man, and he habitually dressed in purple and fine linen, joyously living in splendor every day. And a poor man named Lazarus was laid at his gate, covered with sores, and longing to be fed with the crumbs which were falling from the rich man's table; besides even the dogs were coming and licking his sores. Now the poor man died and was carried away by the angels to Abraham's bosom; and the rich man also died and was buried.

"In Hades he lifted up his eyes, being in torment, and saw Abraham far away and Lazarus in his bosom. And he cried out and said, 'Father Abraham, have mercy on me, and send Lazarus so that he may dip the tip of his finger in water and cool off my tongue, for I am in agony in this flame.' But Abraham said, 'Child, remember that in your life you received your good things, and likewise Lazarus bad things; but now he is being comforted here, and you are in agony. And besides all this, between us and you there is a great chasm fixed, so that those who wish to come over here to you will not be able, and that none may cross over from there to us.' And he said, 'I beg you, father, that you send him to my father's house–for I have five brothers–in order that he may warn them, so that they will not also come to this place of torment.'

"But Abraham said, 'They have Moses and the Prophets; let them hear them.' But he said, 'No, father Abraham, but if someone goes to them from the dead, they will repent.' But he said to him, 'If they do not listen to Moses and the Prophets, they will not be persuaded even if someone rises from the dead.'"

There is a third thing that we need to see about Hades. Jesus tells us about the rich man and Lazarus the beggar, and how they both died and went to Hades. However, we see from the passage above that, according to Jesus, they had very different experiences there. The rich man was in torment, while Lazarus was resting peacefully in Abraham's bosom. Here we see that Hades has two distinct separate parts.

The rich man looked up and saw Lazarus afar off. The upper part of Hades, referred to in Scripture as paradise, is where the souls of the righteous go and are comforted after the death of their physical bodies. In Luke 23:42-43 the thief on the cross saw that Jesus was undeserving of death, and confessed Him as King, as Lord, saying, "Jesus, remember me when you come in your kingdom." Jesus told the repentant thief, "Truly I say to you, today you shall be with Me in Paradise."

The lower part of Hades is where the souls of the unrighteous go and are tormented after the death of their physical bodies. It is not possible to cross over from one part of Hades to the other part of Hades. For the unrighteous, Jesus says that Hades is an inescapable place of torment. Abraham reminded the rich man that he had received his good things during his lifetime and Lazarus had received bad things, but now in Hades, Lazarus is comforted, and the rich man is in agony.

Jesus also tells us how Lazarus was left at the rich man's gate hungry and longing to be fed but received nothing. This should cause us to pause and reflect on how we are living our lives in relation to the poor and needy around us. It is not enough just to claim to be a believer; we must demonstrate our faith by how we treat others.

Finally, in Revelation 20:13-14, we see that Hades is just a temporary holding place for the souls of the dead. "Death and Hades gave up the dead which were in them; and they were judged, every one of them according to their deeds. Then death and Hades were thrown into the lake of fire. This is the second death, the lake of fire."

Hades is a very real place where the souls of the dead are held awaiting final judgment. Hades is a temporary place of torment for the unrighteous, and a temporary place of comfort for the righteous. At the judgment seat, Hades is emptied and then it is thrown into the lake of fire. Its usefulness has been completed.

Chapter 16 Discussion Questions: Life After Death

1. What are two common views of life after death?
2. What three Greek words are translated as 'hell' in the King James Version of the New Testament?
3. What is the Hebrew equivalent of the Greek word Hades?
4. What does Psalm 139:7-8 say about Sheol?
5. What does I Thessalonians 4:16-17 say will happen just before we who are alive and remain are caught up to the Lord?

6. Where do the souls of believers go when they die?
7. What was the difference in the experience of Lazarus and the rich man in Hades?
8. Why were their experiences different?
9. Why couldn't Lazarus go to comfort the rich man?
10. Why wouldn't Abraham send someone from the dead to warn the rich man's brothers?
11. What did Jesus promise the thief on the cross?
12. When will Hades be emptied out and cast into the Lake of Fire?

The Lake of Fire

A s we have already seen, there are three different Greek words that are translated as "hell" in the King James Version of the New Testament. The first of these Greek words is "Hades." We have seen that Hades is a very real place where the souls of the dead are held awaiting final judgment. Hades is a temporary place of torment for the unrighteous, and a temporary place of comfort for the righteous. At the judgment seat, Hades is emptied out and then it is thrown into the lake of fire. Its usefulness has been completed.

The next word translated as "hell" is "Gehenna." In Mathew 10:28 Jesus used the term Gehenna to refer to the place where God is able to destroy both the body and soul. He said, "Don't be afraid of those who kill the body, but are not able to kill the soul. Rather, fear Him who is able to destroy both soul and body in Gehenna" (WEB).

Notice that here Jesus does not talk about the soul being in torment as in Hades. Here Jesus talks about the soul being destroyed, along with the body. In Hades the soul of the unrighteous is tormented after the natural physical body has died. In Gehenna, the soul and the resurrected spiritual body are destroyed.

Jesus tells us in John 5:29, all "will come forth; those who did good deeds to a resurrection of life, those who committed evil deeds to a resurrection of judgment." 1 Corinthians 15:44 says, "It is sown a natural body, it is raised a spiritual body. There is a natural body, there is also a spiritual body." The body that is destroyed in Gehenna is the spiritual body of the resurrection.

Jesus uses the word Gehenna again in Mark 9:43-48 where He says, "It is better for you to enter into life maimed, rather than having your two hands to go into Gehenna, into the unquenchable fire, 'where their worm doesn't die, and the fire is not quenched'" (WEB). He is quoting from Isaiah 66:24 where the Lord says, "As they leave, they will see the dead bodies of the men who have rebelled against Me; for their worm will never die, their fire will never go out, and they will be a horror to all mankind" (WEB).

Here Isaiah describes a scene on the new earth, just outside of the New Jerusalem. As the people leave the New Jerusalem, after worshipping the Lord, they pass by this lake of fire and see the dead bodies of the people who rebelled against the Lord. This lake of fire is the place of eternal fire, the place of eternal punishment, spoken of in Matthew 25 and in Revelation 20, referred to by Jesus in Mark 9 as Gehenna.

In Matthew 25:41-45 Jesus says, "Then He will also say to those on His left, 'Depart from Me, accursed ones, into the eternal fire which has been prepared for the devil and his angels; for I was hungry, and you gave Me nothing to eat; I was thirsty, and you gave Me nothing to drink; I was a stranger, and you did not invite Me in; naked, and you did not clothe Me; sick, and in prison, and you did not visit Me.' Then they themselves also will answer, 'Lord, when did we see You hungry, or thirsty, or a stranger, or naked, or sick, or in prison, and did not take care of You?' Then He will answer them, 'Truly I say to you, to the extent that you did not do it to one of the least of these, you did not do it to Me.' These will go away into eternal punishment, but the righteous into eternal life." Again, this should give us pause to consider how we are living our lives in relation to the poor and needy around us.

Notice that the eternal fire was prepared for the devil and the angels that followed him. In fact, in Revelation 20:10 we read that the devil was "thrown into the lake of fire and sulfur where the beast and the false prophet are, and they will be tormented day and night forever and ever." This Gehenna, the lake of fire, the place of eternal fire, was not created for people, but for the devil and his angels. 2 Peter 3:9 tells us that God does not want any people to perish, "but for all to come to repentance."

However, we see in Revelation 20 that anyone whose name is not found written in the Lamb's book of life is cast into this lake of fire, Gehenna, the place of eternal punishment. God's desire is that none would perish. However, when a person chooses to rebel against God, and refuses to repent, and refuses to listen to the voice of the Lord and obey Him, eventually the righteous God must judge them according to their actions.

This lake of fire, Gehenna, is called the second death because in the lake of fire the bodies and souls of these people that are cast into it are destroyed. This is why Isaiah did not describe the people in the lake of fire as alive and in torment. He only saw the dead spiritual bodies of those that had been resurrected, the corpses, of the unrighteous people that had rebelled against the Lord.

I have not found any place in Scripture that says people will be tormented for eternity. However, the Scriptures are very clear that the souls of the unrighteous will be tormented in Hades until Hades is emptied at the coming judgment. The people that are cast into the lake of fire are destroyed, body and soul, and only their dead carcasses, only their corpses, remain as an eternal reminder of God's righteous judgment.

There is a passage in Revelation 14:9-11 that often causes confusion on this point. This passage says, "If anyone worships the beast and his image, and receives a mark on his forehead or on his hand...he will be tormented with fire and brimstone in the presence of the holy angels and in the presence of the Lamb. And the smoke of their torment goes up forever and ever; they have no rest day and night, those who worship the beast and his image, and whoever receives the mark of his name."

As we saw in Isaiah 66, the lake of fire is "away from" the presence of the Lord. However, in the passage above we see that those that receive the mark of the beast are tormented "in" the presence of the Lord and "in" the presence of the holy angels. Psalm 139:8 says, "If I ascend to heaven, You are there; if I make my bed in Sheol, behold, You are there." The Lord is not only in heaven, He is also there in Hades or Sheol. Therefore, it appears that this torment takes place in Hades in the presence of the Lord and possibly at the judgment seat.

Hebrews 9:27 informs us that, "It is appointed for men to die once and after this comes judgment." Hebrews 10:27 says there is a "terrifying expectation of judgment." Hebrews 10:31 says, "It is a terrifying thing to fall into the hands of the living God." It sounds like the unrighteous will experience another time of torment "in" the presence of the Lord at the coming judgment. However, there is no indication of any person being tormented forever "away from" the Lord in Gehenna, the lake of fire.

We should also notice that this passage says that the smoke of their torment goes up forever and ever. It does not say that they are tormented forever and ever. Also note that the word translated forever and ever is the Greek word "aion." This is not the same as the Greek word translated eternal, "aionios." Aion means eon or ages, a long period of time. As we have seen, Hades is not emptied for the final judgment until after the 1,000 year reign of Christ. It appears, therefore, that those who received the mark of the beast will spend at least 1,000 years in the torment of Hades. That is a long period of time with no rest.

The final word translated as hell is the Greek word "Tartarus." 2 Peter 2:4 says, "God didn't spare angels when they sinned, but cast them down to Tartarus, and committed them to pits of darkness, to be reserved for judgment" (WEB). Tartarus means an abyss. It is a place that God created to hold these rebellious angels until the final judgment.

Let's summarize the meaning of the three Greek words translated as "hell" in the New Testament. Hades is the temporary holding place of the souls of people whose natural physical bodies have died. It has an upper section, paradise, where the souls of the righteous are comforted. It also has a lower section where the souls of the unrighteous are tormented. It is not possible to cross over from one section to the other. When you die your fate is sealed, it cannot be changed.

Gehenna is the final place of eternal punishment that was prepared by God for Satan and the evil spirits that followed him. It is a lake of eternal fire into which the people whose names are not found in the book of life at the judgment seat are cast. Both the resurrected spiritual bodies and the souls of these people are destroyed in this lake of fire. This lake of fire remains on the new earth outside the New Jerusalem, away from the presence of the Lord as an eternal remembrance of God's righteous judgment.

The last word translated as "hell" is Tartarus. It is the abyss where some of the angels that rebelled with Satan are held awaiting their final judgment.

In Matthew 7:21 Jesus says, "Not everyone who says to Me, 'Lord, Lord,' will enter the kingdom of heaven, but only he who does the will of My Father who is in heaven. On that day many will say to Me, 'Lord, Lord, didn't we prophesy in Your name, drive out demons in Your name, and do many miracles in Your name?' Then I will answer them, 'I never knew you! Depart from me, you lawbreakers.'"

Many people will be shocked at the judgment when they learn that everything done out of self-effort and religious duty will be considered lawlessness. Only obedience that issues from a living, loving relationship with Jesus will be of any value. Only those that believe God's promise and live by faith in Jesus will be considered righteous.

Chapter 17 Discussion Questions:
The Lake of Fire

1. The Greek word Gehenna is translated as hell in Matthew 10:28, what place does it refer to?
2. What does it say happens to the soul in Gehenna?
3. What scene does Isaiah describe in Isaiah 66:24?
4. Who was the place of eternal fire prepared for?
5. Who will be tormented forever in the Lake of Fire?
6. What happens to those in Revelation 20 whose names are not found in the book of life?
7. Why is Gehenna, the Lake of Fire, called the second death?
8. Where will people be tormented after death?
9. What does the Greek word 'aion' in Revelation 14:11 actually mean?
10. What value will self-effort and religious duty have at the judgment?

The Great White Throne Judgment

What is going to happen at the coming judgment? What will determine the outcome of this judgment for each person? As we shall see, the answers to these questions may have a tremendous impact on the rest of your life! Let's begin our quest for these answers by turning to one of the last chapters in the last book of the Bible, the book of Revelation.

Revelation 20:11-15 says: "Then I saw a great white throne and Him who sat upon it, from whose presence earth and heaven fled away, and no place was found for them. And I saw the dead, the great and the small, standing before the throne, and books were opened; and another book was opened, which is the book of life; and the dead were judged from the things which were written in the books, according to their deeds. And the sea gave up the dead which were in it, and death and Hades gave up the dead which were in them; and they were judged, every one of them according to their deeds. Then death and Hades were thrown into the lake of fire. This is the second death, the lake of fire. And if anyone's name was not found written in the book of life, he was thrown into the lake of fire."

According to this passage, everyone will be judged based on two things. First, we will be judged by our own works. 2 Corinthians 5:10 says, "For we must all appear before the judgment seat of Christ, so that each one may be recompensed for his deeds in the body, according to what he has done, whether good or bad." These things are written in the "books" that are opened.

This makes clear the importance of what we do while our physical body is still alive, because our actions are being recorded, and we will be judged by those actions. It is important to note that, while we are still living in our physical body, we have the opportunity to change our actions and affect the outcome of our judgment.

This passage in Revelation 20 also makes it clear that there is one other thing that will determine the outcome of the judgment each of us will face. This second thing is even more important than our works. The most critical thing for each of us, according to this passage, is whether our names are found to be written in "the book of life."

In addition to the books being opened that records all of our works, "another book was opened, which was the book of life." Then "anyone not found written in the book of life was thrown into the lake of fire." This lake of fire is referred to as "the second death."

Our physical bodies will have already died. That was the first death. Revelation 20 says that this lake of fire is the second death. This lake of fire is where the Devil, the beast, and the false prophet will be cast, and where they "will be tormented day and night forever and ever" (Rev. 19:20, 20:10). According to Matthew 25:41 and 46 the place of "eternal punishment," "the eternal fire" was "prepared for the devil and his angels." These are spiritual beings with an eternal existence and will therefore be thrown into a place of eternal torment.

Every person needs to be most concerned with what it says in Revelation 20:15; "Anyone not found written in the book of life was thrown into the lake of fire." Anyone whose name is not found in the book of life and is thrown into the lake of fire will experience "the second death." The second death will not kill the physical body. That has already died.

I believe the second death will kill the soul and the resurrected spiritual body. After being judged according to their works, every person that is not found written in the book of life will be thrown into the lake of fire, and will experience the second death, the death that destroys their soul and their resurrected spiritual body.

1 Corinthians 15:42-44 says, "So It is with the resurrection of the dead:...sown a natural body, raised a spiritual body." In Isaiah 66:22-24 God says, "As they leave, they will see the dead bodies of the men who have rebelled against Me; for their worm will never die, their fire will never go out."

Jesus warns in Matthew 10:28: "Don't be afraid of those who kill the body, but are not able to kill the soul. Rather, fear Him who is able to destroy both soul and body in Gehenna" (WEB). This passage makes it clear that the soul is not immortal. It is not eternal. A person's soul can be killed, destroyed by God. If anyone's name is not found written in the book of life, that person will be cast into the lake of fire, the second death. The death that they experience there will be the death of their soul and the death of their resurrected spiritual body.

According to Romans 6:23, "The gift of God is eternal life in Christ Jesus our Lord." 1 John 5:11 confirms this, saying, "And the testimony is this, that God has given us eternal life, and this life is in His Son." These passages make it very clear that eternal life is in Jesus Christ. Apart from Him no one has eternal life. Life that is not eternal does not live forever. Therefore, any person who does not have Christ dwelling in them does not have eternal life, and shall be destroyed, dying in the second death.

Evidence that man is mortal and will not live forever apart from receiving eternal life in Jesus Christ can be seen at the end of the account of the fall of man in the Garden of Eden. Genesis 3:22-24 says: "Then the LORD God said, 'Behold, the man has become like one of Us, knowing good and evil; and now, he might stretch out his hand, and take also from the tree of life, and eat, and live forever'— therefore the LORD God sent him out from the garden of Eden, to

141

cultivate the ground from which he was taken. So He drove the man out; and at the east of the garden of Eden He stationed the cherubim and the flaming sword which turned every direction to guard the way to the tree of life." Until the issue of man's sin was dealt with, God would not allow man to receive eternal life and live forever.

In Exodus 32:33 God says to Moses: "I will erase whoever has sinned against Me from My book" (HCSB). In Psalm 69:28 the psalmist asks God to let those that persecute His righteous ones "be erased from the book of life and not be recorded with the righteous" (HCSB). In Revelation 3:5 Jesus assures His faithful ones, "I will not erase his name from the book of life, and I will confess his name before My Father and before His angels."

It is apparent from these passages that everyone's name is originally written in the book of life. However, those that have sinned against God will have their names erased from the book of life. This is why Jesus' death on the cross was so important. By His death, Jesus made purification for our sins. Hebrews 1:3 says, "When He had made purification of sins, He sat down at the right hand of the Majesty on high."

All of those that believe God raised Jesus from the dead and confess Jesus as Lord, submitting to Jesus as God's ultimate authority, receive forgiveness of sins in Him. Romans 10:8-10 says, "The word of faith which we are preaching, that if you confess with your mouth Jesus as Lord, and believe in your heart that God raised Him from the dead, you will be saved; for with the heart a person believes, resulting in righteousness, and with the mouth he confesses, resulting in salvation." Colossians 1:13-14 says: "For He rescued us from the domain of darkness, and transferred us to the kingdom of His beloved Son, in whom we have redemption, the forgiveness of sins."

In Matthew 26:28 Jesus says: "For this is My blood of the covenant, which is poured out for many for the forgiveness of sins." Luke 24:46-47 says: "Thus it is written, that the Christ would suffer and rise again from the dead the third day, and that repentance for forgiveness of sins would be proclaimed in His name to all the nations, beginning from Jerusalem."

I John 3:5 tells us that Christ appeared "in order to take away sins." In promising to make a new covenant with His people, God says, "And this is my covenant with them when I take away their sins" (Romans 11:27).

This forgiveness of sins that we can have by faith in Jesus the Christ prevents our names from being erased from the book of life, because the blood of Jesus does not just cover up our sins, it takes away our sins. If we have received forgiveness of our sins by faith in Jesus, we can be assured that our names will not be erased from the book of life and that we will not be among those that experience the second death by being cast into the lake of fire.

Works of the law, and good works, cannot save us from this second death. Only faith in Jesus, resulting in our confession of Him as Lord, and our total submission to Him as God's authority in heaven and on earth, can save us from the second death. Our works will only affect the outcome of the initial judgment that we all shall face when we stand before the great throne of God's judgment, where we will receive recompense based on the things that we have done, whether good or bad.

Unbelievers have a much greater concern than just being judged according to their works. If they have not believed in Jesus and submitted to Him as Lord, they will not have availed themselves of the benefit of His redeeming work on the cross. They are therefore still in their sins, and their names will have been erased from the book of life. Their destiny, apart from believing in Jesus and submitting to Him, is the second death, the lake of fire.

Unbelievers will only have the opportunity to repent and come to faith in Jesus as long as their physical body is alive. As soon as they experience the first death, the death of their physical body, it is too late. Their destiny is sealed. The second death has become inevitable for them. For this reason, I implore you, if you have never obeyed the gospel, allow yourself, right now, to be persuaded of the truth as it is in Jesus.

Remember, the one thing that will determine if we suffer the second death at the great white throne judgment is whether or not our name is found written in the book of life. Only if we have received forgiveness of our sins by faith in Jesus, can we be assured that our names will not be erased from the book of life.

The other thing we need to remember is that we can never please God in our own strength, working according to our own understanding and our own wisdom. Only Jesus Christ, by the power of His Spirit that indwells every true believer, can please God. He does this by strengthening us and enabling us to live lives of obedience to the leading of the Holy Spirit. If we have the Spirit of Christ, we must allow that Spirit to lead us and empower us to live a life of total submission to Jesus Christ as Lord. Only a life of loving God and loving others as ourselves will please Him. Only these works, done by the equipping and empowering of the indwelling Spirit of Christ, will stand and receive a reward.

How is it with you? Do you have confidence to stand in that inevitable day of the coming judgment at the great white throne?

Chapter 18 Discussion Questions:
The Great White Throne Judgment

1. Who is sitting on the great white throne?
2. Who is being judged?
3. According to what were they being judged?
4. What was the other book that was opened?
5. What happened to death and Hades?

6. What happened to anyone whose name was not found written in the book of life?

7. What evidence is there in Scripture that the soul is not immortal?

8. How and why is anyone's name removed from the book of life?

9. What prevents our names from being erased from the book of life?

10. What can save us from the second death?

11. How can we please God?

Test Yourself

⟶

The one and only authoritative book accepted by virtually all those that claim to be Christians is the Bible.
Most Christians believe that the Bible, which I shall refer to
here as the Scriptures, is infallible in its original writing. It
is for this reason that I, as one that claims to be a Christian,
am extremely troubled whenever I read a passage in the
Scriptures that is inconsistent with what I observe in
Christianity or among professing Christians today.

One such passage has to do with the sheer numbers
of people that claim to be Christians. Tens of millions of
people in the world today and throughout history claim to be
Christians. However, the Scriptures say in Matthew 7:13-14:
"Enter through the narrow gate; for the gate is wide and the
way is broad that leads to destruction, and there are many
who enter through it. For the gate is small and the way is
narrow that leads to life, and there are few who find it."

If in fact the Scriptures are true, then the number
of Christians in relation to the total population must be
"few." According to *Strong's Exhaustive Concordance*, the
Greek word translated as "few" in this passage has the lit-
eral meaning of "puny in number." In 2015 75% of the
adults polled in the United States claimed to be Christians.
Obviously, there is a significant inconsistency between the
Scriptures and what professing Christians in the United
States are claiming.

In order to determine if what all of these professing
Christians were claiming was true, I looked to the Scriptures
for more information that would enable me to identify the
cause of this apparent inconsistency. Do the Scriptures have

some sort of standard or test that would enable any professing Christian to know for sure if they really are a Christian?

No one wants to be deceived. Everyone who claims to be a Christian should want to know with assurance whether or not they really are a genuine Christian. Is there a test, and if so, do we pass this test?

Reading in the same chapter in Matthew, Jesus continues speaking in 7:21-23 saying: "Not everyone who says to Me, 'Lord, Lord!' will enter the kingdom of heaven, but only the one who does the will of My Father in heaven. On that day many will say to Me, 'Lord, Lord, didn't we prophesy in Your name, drive out demons in Your name, and do many miracles in Your name?' Then I will announce to them, 'I never knew you! Depart from Me, you lawbreakers!'" (HCSB). Here we see that many of those who claim to have done all manner of great things in the name of the Lord will seek entrance into the kingdom of heaven, but Jesus will say to them in that day, "Depart from me, I never knew you."

This passage makes it clear that there are certain requirements to gain entrance into the kingdom of heaven. One of these requirements is that we do the will of His Father. Another is that Jesus knows us. It is also clear that doing all manner of great works for the Lord will not be sufficient to qualify us to gain entrance into the kingdom of heaven.

What does it mean to do the will of His Father? Each of us has a choice. We can do what we want, or we can do what someone else wants. If someone of greater authority than ourselves asks us to do something, we can choose to do what they ask, that is obedience; or we can refuse to do what they ask and do what we want, that is rebellion. To do the will of His Father, then, is simply to obey Him.

In Matthew 28:18-19 Jesus met with His disciples and spoke to them just before He ascended into heaven saying: "All authority has been given to Me in heaven and on earth. Go therefore and make disciples of all nations." Jesus, the only person who had lived a life without sin, was crucified, being nailed to a cross. He died and was buried. Then on the third day God, by the power of the resurrection, raised Jesus up, never to die again. By the power of the resurrection from the dead, God placed His seal of approval on Jesus' life and death, and gave all authority unto Him, making Him both Lord and Christ (Acts 2:22-40; Romans 1:4).

This is exactly what Peter preached on the day of Pentecost. Peter said in Acts 2:32-33: "God has resurrected this Jesus. We are all witnesses of this. Therefore, since He has been exalted to the right hand of God and has received from the Father the promised Holy Spirit, He has poured out what you both see and hear" (HCSB). Peter continues in verse 36 saying: "Therefore let all the house of Israel know for certain that God has made Him both Lord and Christ—this Jesus whom you crucified."

This is the gospel message, the message of good news that Peter, Paul, and all the apostles preached throughout the book of Acts. They preached the kingdom of God and Jesus, the Christ, as Lord. In Philippians 2:9-11, Paul tells us: "For this reason God highly exalted Him and gave Him the name that is above every name, so that at the name of Jesus every knee should bow—of those who are in heaven and on earth and under the earth—and every tongue should confess that Jesus Christ is Lord, to the glory of God the Father" (HCSB). This is the Father's will.

Paul declares in Romans 10:8-10: "This is the message of faith that we proclaim: If you confess with your mouth, 'Jesus is Lord,' and believe in your heart that God raised Him from the dead, you will be saved. One believes with the heart, resulting in righteousness, and one confesses with the mouth, resulting in salvation" (HCSB). This message of faith that Paul and the other apostles proclaimed was in total agreement with the will of God. This message is altogether about the Lordship of Jesus, about the authority that God the Father has given unto Him, and whether we will willingly, gladly submit to His authority, confessing Jesus as Lord.

The Scriptures tell us in Acts 5:29-32: "But Peter and the apostles answered, 'We must obey God rather than men. The God of our fathers raised up Jesus, whom you had put to death by hanging Him on a cross. He is the one whom God exalted to His right hand as a Prince and a Savior, to grant repentance to Israel, and forgiveness of sins. And we are witnesses of these things; and *so is* the Holy Spirit, whom God has given to those who obey Him.'" God gives His Holy Spirit to those that obey the "ruler" that He has appointed and exalted to His right hand. The Father's will is that we totally submit to Jesus the Christ as Lord. We cannot really know Him if we do not know Him as Lord.

In Matthew 10:32 Jesus says: "Everyone who will acknowledge Me before men, I will also acknowledge him before My Father in heaven. But whoever denies Me before men, I will also deny him before My Father in heaven" (HCSB). The word translated "deny" here actually means to not confess. Paul talked in Romans 10 about the necessity of confessing with the mouth "Jesus is Lord" resulting in salvation. Here Jesus says that if we confess Him as Lord before men, He will confess us as His own to His Father in heaven.

This brings us back to the passage in Matthew 7:21-23 where people were addressing Jesus by His title of Lord, but were not submitted to Him as their Lord. Jesus refused to confess that He knew them. He denied them because even though they did all manner of great works in His name, they were not submitted to Him as Lord. If they were, Jesus would have acknowledged that He knew them. He did not. He denied knowing them.

Psalm 81:11-15 says: "My people did not listen to My voice, And Israel did not obey Me. So I gave them over to the stubbornness of their heart, to walk in their own devices. Oh that My people would listen to Me, that Israel would walk in My ways! I would quickly subdue their enemies and turn My hand against their adversaries. Those who hate the LORD would pretend obedience to Him."

God gives His Spirit to those that obey His authority, Jesus, the Christ. Romans 8:9 states: "If anyone does not have the Spirit of Christ, he does not belong to Him." This is very clear, and it is very consistent with the passages that we have looked at. If anyone does not obey God, fully submitting to His authority, Jesus Christ the Lord, they do not belong to Him. If you obey the message of the gospel, believing that God raised Jesus from the dead, and confessing "Jesus is Lord", you will receive the Holy Spirit. When you receive the Spirit, you belong to Christ, and He will confess you before His Father.

2 Corinthians 13:5 challenges everyone that claims to be a Christian to: "Test yourselves *to see* if you are in the faith; examine yourselves! Or do you not recognize this about yourselves, that Jesus Christ is in you—unless indeed you fail the test?" 2 Corinthians 3:17 declares: "Now the Lord is the Spirit, and where the Spirit of the Lord is, *there* is liberty." If Jesus Christ, as the Spirit, does not dwell within your spirit, you are not in the faith. If you don't pass the test, if you don't have the Spirit of Christ in you, you are not His, you are not a genuine Christian.

I John 5:11-13 says: "And this is the testimony: That God has given us eternal life, and this life is in His Son. The one who has the Son has life. The one who does not have the Son of God does not have life. I have written these things to you who believe in the name of the Son of God, so that you may know that you have eternal life" (HCSB). God wants us to know for sure if we are genuine Christians. However, He does not want our assurance based on what some person might have told us.

You might have been raised as a Christian. You might be a member of a church. You might even be in fulltime Christian ministry. However, Scripture makes it very clear, it does not matter what you have done for the Lord, if His Spirit is not in you, you are not in the faith and you fail the test, you are not a genuine Christian.

I urge you not to rely on any assurance that any other person has ever given to you that you are a Christian. No one can know your heart, not your parents, not your pastor, not your Sunday-school teacher, or any evangelist. No other person can know for sure if you are saved. Only you and God can know for sure. And remember, God wants you to know. He has provided several ways for you to know for sure. He has even provided a simple test to see if you are indeed in the faith.

Until we all appear before the Judgment Seat, only you and God know if you are truly a Christian. How can you know for sure? Romans 8:16 assures genuine believers that: "The Spirit Himself testifies with our spirit that we are children of God." Romans 5:5 says: "the love of God has been poured out within our hearts through the Holy Spirit who was given to us." I John 3:14 affirms: "We know that we have passed from death to life because we love our brothers. The one who does not love remains in death" (HCSB).

Do you pass the test? Do you have Jesus Christ as the Spirit indwelling in your spirit? Does the Spirit bear witness with your spirit that you are a child of God? Has God's love been poured out in your heart? Do you love the brothers in Christ?

No one wants to be deceived. We all want to know the truth. We want to know for sure if we really are genuine Christians. To know for sure, all we have to do is take this simple test and honestly assess the results. How confident are you that Jesus will confess you before His Father?

Hebrews 5:9, speaking of Jesus, says: "He became the source of eternal salvation for all who obey Him" (HCSB). Have you obeyed Jesus? Have you done the will of the Father? Have you bowed the knee and received Jesus as your Lord and Master? Have you confessed Jesus as Lord before men?

If you are reading this, you still have time. Right now, today, believing that God raised Jesus from the dead, you can bow the knee and receive Jesus as Lord, confessing Him before men, and know with the assurance that only God Himself can give you, that Jesus will confess you before His Father in heaven.

If you do this, as a genuine believer, you will have the opportunity to experience the Spirit Himself bearing witness with your spirit that you are indeed a child of God!

Charter 19 Discussion Questions: Test Yourself

1. What does it mean when it says that there are few that find the way that leads to life?
2. How do you feel about being deceived?
3. Do you want to know for sure if you are a genuine Christian?
4. What are some of the requirements for gaining entrance into the kingdom of heaven?
5. What does it mean to do the will of the Father?
6. What is the Father's will?
7. What response did Jesus give to those who had done all manner of great things in His name?
8. Who will Jesus acknowledge before His Father in heaven?
9. What is the test that Paul challenges believers to take?
10. How can you know if you pass the test?

Bowing the Knee

Jesus Christ is unique. He is one of a kind. Revelation 17:14 declares that Jesus is "Lord of lords and King of kings." In Mathew 28:18 Jesus declares that, "All authority has been given to Me in heaven and on earth."

In John 14:6 Jesus said: "I am the way, and the truth, and the life; no one comes to the Father but through Me." Notice Jesus did not say "I am a way, a truth, and a life." No, He said He was THE way, THE truth, and THE life.

There is no other way to God. Jesus is the way. No man can come to God except by Jesus. Jesus is the one unique way to God.

There are people all over the world claiming they have found another way to God. These are all liars and false prophets. Not one of them can bring you to God. Jesus is the only way to God.

Jesus said: "I am the truth." The word truth here does not mean a fact or a correct understanding of something. The word truth here means reality. Jesus is the one reality in this world. Everything outside of Him is just a shadow, a vapor with no substance. Jesus is the reality. He is the only one of genuine substance.

Jesus said: "I am the life." Every person that has ever lived on this earth has had a physical life and a soul life. Their body had life, and their soul had life. But not one of them had God's eternal life unless they had believed and had received Jesus, the Christ, as the Lord, into their spirit. Jesus is eternal life. I John 5:12 declares: "He who has the Son has the life; he who does not have the Son of God does not have the life."

You may have life in your body. You may have life in your soul. But your spirit is dead, unless you have received Jesus as your Lord, and He has quickened, given life to, your spirit. If you do not have Jesus, you do not have life. You are dead even while you live in your physical body.

On the last day, at the Judgment Seat of Christ, after Satan, the great deceiver, has been cast into the lake of fire, everyone will bow the knee and confess Jesus Christ as Lord. With Satan cast into the lake of fire, all deception will be gone, and everyone will see clearly that Jesus is King of kings and Lord of lords. All will see that it is to Him alone that each one must give account of themselves as to how they have lived during their time on this earth.

Romans 14:10-12 proclaims: "For we will all stand before the judgment seat of Christ. For it is written, 'As I live,' says the Lord, 'to me every knee will bow. Every tongue will confess to God.' So then each one of us will give account of himself to God" (WEB). This is inevitable. God says it will happen. Every knee will bow. Every tongue will confess.

The good news is that we don't have to wait until the last day. We don't have to wait until we are standing before the Judgment Seat of Christ to see the truth of who Jesus is. God, in the Bible, the Scriptures, has revealed to us who this Jesus is. God is speaking through His apostles and prophets, declaring to any who will listen, that Jesus Christ is Lord of all.

Jesus said in Matthew 28:18: "All authority has been given to Me in heaven and on earth." Peter proclaimed in Acts 2:36: "Therefore let all the house of Israel know for certain that God has made Him both Lord and Christ—this Jesus whom you crucified." Paul states in Romans 10:8-10: "This is the message of faith that we proclaim: If you confess with your mouth, 'Jesus is Lord,' and believe in your heart that God raised Him from the dead, you will be saved. One believes with the heart, resulting in righteousness, and one confesses with the mouth, resulting in salvation" (HCSB).

Those that choose to listen to this message about Jesus the Christ, and by hearing, believe that God raised Him from the dead, never to die again, and confess Jesus as Lord, will be saved. If you simply have an ear to hear what God is speaking about Jesus, and if you have a heart to believe and obey, and submit to His authority, you will be saved.

In Philippians 2:5-11 Paul exhorts: "Have this mind, which was also in Christ Jesus, who, existing in the form of God, didn't consider equality with God a thing to be grasped, but emptied himself, taking the form of a servant, being made in the likeness of men. And being found in human form, he humbled himself, becoming obedient to death, yes, the death of the cross. Therefore God also highly exalted him, and gave to him the name which is above every name; that at the name of Jesus every knee should bow, of those in heaven, those on earth, and those under the earth, and that every tongue should confess that Jesus Christ is Lord, to the glory of God the Father" (WEB).

Here, unlike the passage that we read from Romans 14, where it said everyone "will" bow the knee, here it says everyone "should" bow the knee. This passage is not referring to the last day at the judgment seat. This passage is referring to right now. Upon hearing that God has highly exalted Jesus and given Him a name above every name, everyone should bow the knee and confess that Jesus Christ is Lord. Now, today, bowing the knee to Jesus is not mandated by God, it is something that those who believe in Him choose freely to do.

Those that, believing, freely choose to humble themselves and submit to Jesus as God's ultimate authority, confessing Him as Lord, will be saved. They receive Him into their spirit as their life. They receive the forgiveness of sins. They enter into His kingdom of light and into an untold multitude of blessings both in this life and throughout eternity.

Perhaps the greatest blessing is that these genuine believers know Him and are known by Him. Jesus said in Matthew 7:21-23: "Not everyone who says to Me, 'Lord, Lord!' will enter the kingdom of heaven, but only the one who does the will of My Father in heaven. On that day many will say to Me, 'Lord, Lord, didn't we prophesy in Your name, drive out demons in Your name, and do many miracles in Your name?' Then I will announce to them, 'I never knew you! Depart from Me, you lawbreakers!'" (HCSB). What a blessing it will be to hear Jesus acknowledge, to His Father in heaven, that He knows us.

Genuine, born-again believers enter into an intimate loving relationship with Jesus their Lord. They have peace with God and their joy is full. The fruit of the Spirit, love, joy, peace, patience, kindness, goodness, faith, gentleness, and self-control begins to be produced in their lives (Galatians 5:22-23).

You can freely choose today, if you have an ear to hear what the Spirit is speaking concerning this Jesus, to humble yourself before God, and bow the knee, confessing Jesus as Lord. Everyone will eventually bow the knee and confess Jesus as Lord. Some will refuse to do it until they come before the Judgment Seat of Christ when they will have no choice. And, because they will have no choice, they will receive no benefit.

Those that choose today to listen to the message about this Jesus, and allow themselves to be persuaded as to the truth of the gospel message, and upon believing, humble themselves, and in obedience confessing Jesus as Lord, will be saved. Because they choose freely to believe and obey, they will be rewarded freely. Jesus said in John 10:10, "I came that they may have life, and have *it* abundantly."

Jesus does not just give us life. He gives us life in abundance. God freely pours out His Spirit upon all those that obey Him now in this life. In John 14:21 Jesus tells us, "Every man who knows my commandments and obeys them,

this is the man who really loves me" (Phillips). 1 Corinthians
2:9 promises: "Things which eye has not seen and ear has
not heard, and which have not entered the heart of man, all
that God has prepared for those who love Him."

We cannot even begin to imagine all that God has prepared for those that love Him. This is one very important
reason why God gives His Spirit to those that obey Him, so
we might know the things that God has prepared for us. 1
Corinthians 2:12 states, we have received: "the Spirit who
is from God, so that we may know the things freely given
to us by God." God is not stingy but gives generously to all
those that are His. Not only is He generous, but He wants
every true believer to know what He has given us in Christ.
Even more important, He wants every true believer to freely
avail themselves, right now, of all that He has given us in
Christ Jesus our Lord!

Your eternal destiny, as well as your daily living, depends
on when you bow the knee and confess Jesus as Lord. As
to the time at which you choose to do it, the choice is yours.

You can do it now in this life and enjoy all the blessings
that go with being a child of God, both now and throughout
eternity, or you can wait and do it at the coming judgment,
before the Judgment Seat of Christ.

One thing is certain. Everyone will eventually bow the
knee and confess Jesus as Lord. That I can guarantee.

The only question that remains is, "When will you?"

Charter 20 Discussion Questions:
Bowing the Knee

1. What are the ways in which people can come to God?
2. What is the meaning of the word 'truth'?
3. How does one go about receiving eternal life?
4. When will everyone see clearly that Jesus is King of
   kings and Lord of lords?

5. When will everyone bow the knee and confess to God that Jesus is Lord?

6. Does everyone have to wait until the last day at the judgment seat to confess Christ as Lord?

7. What difference will there be in our reward if we confess Jesus as Lord now or at the last day?

8. What one thing is certain?

Correspondence may be addressed to the author at:
thepureword@yahoo.com